THE BEST OF
BEARD
Great Recipes from a Great Cook

THE BEST OF
BEARD
Great Recipes from a Great Cook

by James Beard
Illustrated by Pat Stewart

Golden Press/New York
Western Publishing Company, Inc.
Racine, Wisconsin

CONTENTS

FOREWORD

I've been cooking for a great many years now, and I've written more than a few books on the subject. But it was not too long ago that a friend of mine asked a very sensible question. "Why," he asked, "do you people who write cookbooks always tell the reader to do something in just one way and no other? You know as well as I do that any cook worth his salt will always make some changes, either because of a personal preference or because some of the ingredients just aren't handy. Besides, we all like to experiment!"

To answer my friend's complaint, I suppose I'd have to say that those of us who have made a business out of cooking and writing about it usually have experimented for years, and when we get a dish exactly the way we like it, we figure that this is the way it should be and no back talk. Having digested my friend's complaint, I think we're wrong, because after all, what is a cook without an independent imagination—and where is the fun unless you experiment? So I'm going to break one of the rules of the trade here. I'm going to tell you some of the secrets of improvisation. Just remember—it's always a good idea to follow the directions exactly the first time you try a recipe. But from then on, you're on your own.

If a recipe calls for liquid or stock, use any broth you may have on hand: meat broth, chicken or game stock, vegetable broths left over from cooking vegetables, tomato juice, thinned-down tomato puree or tomato sauce, any other vegetable juices, or a combination of any of these.

Wines and liquors used as part of the liquid in a recipe add flavor to many dishes, particularly those using meats or fowl. If the basic food in the casserole is delicately flavored, however, go easy on wine or liquor, or you may drown all other taste. And remember that just because a little wine is good in a dish, a great deal will not necessarily be better.

Many meats go well with fruit juices; let your taste buds be your guide. Tomato puree, diluted with a little tomato juice or red wine, makes an excellent liquid for many casseroles. If you're using canned tomato sauce as an added dressing to serve with some meat or vegetable dish, add a little sugar, salt, freshly ground black pepper and butter to it while it's heating. Taste for seasoning.

In changing ingredients in the meat or fish category, a simple rule to follow is to substitute something similar. If the casserole calls for a smoked meat, try to substitute some other variety of smoked meat, for generally the smoky flavor is the taste that should be retained in these dishes. If the meat is delicately flavored, use something equally delicate in its place. If it's heavy and rich, select a rich substitute for it.

As for fish, substitute one shellfish for another, a light fish for one that's delicate, a meaty fish for one that's heavy. Of course, there are many exceptions to this general rule, but they must be discovered by experimentation.

With vegetables as with meats, try to substitute a similar item. For example, many recipes call for shallots. Shallots are small reddish bulbs of the onion family. In many parts of the country they aren't available, although freeze-dried ones are becoming easy to find. In some areas, such as New Orleans, scallions or small green onions are called shallots. You may substitute green onions or any other member of the onion family for shallots, though the flavor won't be duplicated exactly.

Seasonings, herbs and spices are items to be handled with great discrimination. They can make or ruin a dish, and their overuse, along with overcooking, is one of the great faults of beginners. Be cautious with herbs. Better too little than too much. Use bay leaf with discretion; its flavor can be overpowering. Too much thyme gives a bitter tang. Many people find sage indigestible or just plain dislike it. It's better to omit it entirely, but if you must use it, use it sparingly. Rosemary is another herb that some people try to avoid. You can use a little oregano or summer savory instead. But be careful with oregano, for it has a bold flavor. It's often better combined with other herbs. There is no substitute for tarragon, and this herb is something every cook should have on hand.

As for the old standbys salt and pepper, they too need special attention from the cook. Strangely enough, most people undersalt. Taste if you're not sure. I find coarse salt, either Malden sea salt or kosher salt, the best. As for pepper, always use freshly ground black pepper. It alone has the full spicy tang pepper should have. Buy a pepper mill; it's a lifelong investment.

As a matter of fact, this is a good rule of thumb for the cook: Beware of false economies! Good food is a result of the best ingredients in combination. As you go along, you'll find ways to economize without sacrificing quality. Always remember that saving a few pennies on a minor ingredient only to ruin a good piece of meat, for instance, is poor judgment—and the meal that will emerge will certainly show it!

The most important thing is your attitude toward preparing a meal. Relax and enjoy cooking it, and then enjoy eating it, savoring each mouthful and appreciating each new flavor. You'll find that in no time at all, the ideas you'll have for creating your own specialties will clamor for expression.

1
APPETIZERS

CURRIED ALMONDS

---

1 pound shelled almonds   1 teaspoon curry powder
1 clove garlic   Salt to taste
½ cup olive oil

Blanch the almonds in boiling water and remove the skins. Place them in a flat baking pan with the garlic, olive oil and curry powder. Shake well to coat the almonds. Roast in a preheated 350° oven for 25 to 35 minutes or until the almonds are crisp and lightly browned. Sprinkle with salt and add more curry powder if necessary.

CALCUTTAS

---

12 large prunes   Chutney
    Port, water or half and half   6 strips bacon, halved

Soak prunes overnight in port. Drain and dry them. Remove the pits and fill with chutney. Wrap each prune with a piece of bacon and fasten with a wooden pick. Broil until the bacon is crisp.

BROILED PRUNES

---

12 large prunes   6 strips bacon, halved
    Sherry or hot water

Plump prunes in sherry. Remove the pits. Wrap each prune securely with a piece of bacon and fasten with a wooden pick. Broil until the bacon is crisp.

CHEESE PUFFS

¼ cup butter
¾ cup hot water
¾ cup flour
2 eggs

½ cup grated Cheddar cheese
1 teaspoon salt
Dash cayenne pepper

Combine butter and hot water and bring to a boil. Mix in flour all at once and stir quickly until the dough is a solid ball and leaves the sides of the pan. Remove from the fire and beat in 1 egg. Add the second egg and beat until glossy and thoroughly blended. Finally, beat in cheese, salt and cayenne.

Drop by teaspoonfuls onto a buttered baking sheet. Bake in a preheated 375° oven until puffy, well browned and crisp, about 25 to 30 minutes.

Makes about 24 puffs.

CHEESE MATCHES

Prepare a rich pastry or puff paste. Roll it out fairly thin. Dot with butter and sprinkle copiously with grated imported Swiss, Cheddar or Parmesan cheese. Sprinkle the cheese with freshly ground black pepper, a little dry mustard and a tiny dash of cayenne pepper. With a sharp knife, cut into thin matchlike strips and arrange carefully on a baking sheet. Bake in a preheated 400° oven for about 15 minutes or until the pastry is crisp and the cheese melted and golden. Cool and arrange on a plate.

EGGS A LA RUSSE

6 hard-cooked eggs
Shredded greens
¾ cup Mayonnaise (page 153)
3 tablespoons chili sauce
2 teaspoons grated onion

2 teaspoons chopped parsley
Salt to taste
Stuffed green olives, sliced
Capers
Caviar (optional)

Split eggs in half and arrange them, yolks down, on shredded greens. Mix mayonnaise, chili sauce, onion, parsley and salt. Pour over eggs. Decorate with sliced olives and capers. If you really want to celebrate, top each egg with a spoonful of caviar.

Serves 6.

RAW VEGETABLE BOWL WITH DIPPING SAUCES

This bowl should be nice to look at as well as to dip into. Arrange the vegetables in a handsome, appetizing pattern on top of another bowl of crushed ice to keep them crisp, or place cracked ice in the vegetable bowl when you serve it. Make a selection of raw vegetables: celery sticks, tomato wedges, radishes, little green onions, green and red pepper rings, new asparagus tips and long strips of Belgian endive. Have a large selection of ripe olives that have been soaked in oil and garlic for an hour or so before serving. Place the dipping sauces (any or all) in small bowls around the vegetables.

Green Dipping Sauce

½ cup chopped spinach
¼ cup chopped parsley
½ teaspoon salt
½ teaspoon freshly ground
   black pepper

¼ cup finely chopped chives
   or onions
1 cup Mayonnaise (page 153),
   thinned with a little
   light cream

Combine ingredients and beat well. Chill thoroughly before serving.

Makes about 1½ cups.

Braunschweiger Dipping Sauce

½ pound high-quality
    braunschweiger (liverwurst)
1 package (3 ounces)
    cream cheese
1 tablespoon grated onion
1 tablespoon finely chopped
    gherkin

2 teaspoons prepared
    hot mustard
Sweet or dairy sour cream
2 hard-cooked egg yolks,
    chopped
Paprika

Mash the braunschweiger; cream with cream cheese, onion, gherkin, mustard and enough cream to make a dipping consistency. Garnish with egg yolks and paprika.

Makes 1½ cups.

Mustard Dipping Sauce

1 cup dairy sour cream
¼ cup Dijon mustard
½ teaspoon dry mustard
¼ cup capers

2 teaspoons lemon juice
Salt to taste
Chopped chives
Chopped parsley

To the sour cream add Dijon mustard, dry mustard, capers and lemon juice. Blend well, salt to taste and sprinkle heavily with chives and parsley. Chill before serving.

Makes 1½ cups.

Olive-Nut Dipping Sauce

1 cup dairy sour cream
¼ cup chopped ripe olives
¼ cup chopped pimiento-stuffed
    green olives
¼ cup chopped toasted almonds
    and filberts, mixed

Salt and freshly ground
    black pepper to taste
1 tablespoon chopped chives
Capers
Finely chopped pimiento

To the sour cream add olives and almond-filbert mixture. Season to taste with salt and pepper. Beat in chives. Garnish with capers and pimiento.

Makes 1½ cups.

GENTLEMAN'S RELISH

½ cup olive oil
3 medium-size zucchini,
  peeled and sliced
1 large eggplant,
  peeled and diced
  Seasoned flour
1 large onion, chopped
1 clove garlic, crushed
3 medium tomatoes, peeled,
  seeded and chopped
1 teaspoon dry mustard
1 teaspoon oregano
  Salt and freshly ground
  black pepper to taste
  Lettuce
  Lemon wedges

In large, heavy skillet, heat olive oil. Dredge zucchini and eggplant in flour; add to oil with onion and garlic. Cook over low flame until soft and well blended. Add tomatoes, mustard and oregano. Simmer until dish has the appearance of a thick vegetable stew, 10 to 15 minutes. Season with salt and pepper to taste. Chill; stir before serving. Place on a bed of lettuce and garnish with lemon wedges.

Serves 6.

CELERY STUFFED WITH RED CAVIAR

  Pascal celery
1 cup cream cheese
⅓ cup grated onion
⅓ cup chopped parsley
⅓ cup red caviar
  Salt and freshly ground
  black pepper to taste
  Watercress
  Plain celery hearts

Stuff Pascal celery, cut in 1-inch lengths, with mixture of cream cheese creamed with onion, parsley and caviar. Season to taste with salt and pepper. Arrange stuffed celery on a plate with watercress and plain celery hearts. If possible, rest the plate on a bowl of ice.

Makes about 50 pieces.

STUFFED ARTICHOKES

4 large artichokes
¼ cup dry bread crumbs
¼ cup grated Parmesan cheese
½ cup chopped parsley
¼ cup chopped chives

1 tablespoon grated onion
½ clove garlic, grated
¼ cup butter, melted
¼ cup olive oil

Wash artichokes and cut off about ½ inch from leaf tips. Trim stem ends level so artichokes will stand. Combine bread crumbs with cheese, parsley, chives, onion, garlic and butter. Blend and press mixture well down within side leaves and into and across tops of artichokes. Stand them in an earthenware casserole with about ½ inch of water in the bottom. Dribble oil over them. Cover and bake in a preheated 325° oven for 1½ hours or until they are thoroughly tender and the leaves pull away easily.

Serves 4.

ONIONS A LA GRECQUE

36 small white onions
½ cup olive or peanut oil
1 clove garlic
2 cups water
½ cup wine vinegar
1 teaspoon tarragon
1 teaspoon salt

1 teaspoon dry mustard
1 teaspoon mustard seed
1 teaspoon freshly ground
  black pepper
2 cloves
½ cup sultana raisins
  Chopped parsley

In large skillet, place onions with oil, garlic, water, vinegar, tarragon, salt, mustard, mustard seed, pepper and cloves. Bring to a boil; reduce heat and simmer until just tender. Add raisins. Simmer for another 3 to 4 minutes. Chill thoroughly and serve with parsley sprinkled over the top.

Serves 6.

ONION RINGS

½ cup minced parsley
¾ cup Mayonnaise (page 153)
1 Brioche Loaf (page 165) or
   1 loaf egg bread, thinly
   sliced

Salt to taste
7 small white onions,
   thinly sliced

These are monotonous to make, but they're well worth the trouble. The mind of man has never devised a better hors d'oeuvre.

Be sure parsley isn't wet: Wash and dry well in advance and crisp in refrigerator before mincing. Spread ¼ cup mayonnaise on a plate or platter. Cut bread slices into rounds with small-sized biscuit cutter. Spread rounds with remaining mayonnaise and sprinkle with salt. Make sandwiches of 2 rounds with a slice of onion as filling; press each one. Holding each sandwich in your fingers like a wheel, run edge through mayonnaise on plate and then through parsley. Arrange sandwiches on piece of waxed paper, lay another piece of paper on top, wrap well and chill for several hours before serving.

Serves 6.

MUSHROOMS ON TOAST

1 pound mushrooms (whole if
   small, sliced if large)
5 tablespoons butter
   Salt and freshly ground
   black pepper to taste
   Dash Worcestershire sauce

4 tablespoons Madeira or
   sherry wine
4 slices toast, buttered
   Chopped parsley
   Chopped green onion

Sauté mushrooms in butter. When just tender, add salt and pepper, Worcestershire sauce and wine. Serve on hot buttered toast and sprinkle lavishly with parsley and onion.

Serves 4.

STUFFED MUSHROOMS

---

36 medium-size mushrooms
2 cloves garlic, chopped
1 cup toasted bread crumbs
½ cup grated Parmesan cheese
1 egg, well beaten
2 tablespoons olive oil

Salt and freshly ground
  black pepper to taste
Chopped parsley
Butter
1 cup dry white wine
6 slices buttered toast
Grated Parmesan cheese

Chop stems of mushrooms. Combine with the garlic, bread crumbs, cheese, egg and oil. Season to taste with salt and pepper. Stuff mushroom caps with mixture, sprinkle with parsley, dot with butter and arrange in baking pan. Pour in wine. Bake in a preheated 400° oven for 15 minutes. Serve on toast, with a sprinkling of cheese.

Serves 6.

MUSHROOMS WITH SNAIL BUTTER

---

24 large mushroom caps
½ cup butter

6 slices hot toast
Snail Butter (below)

Sauté mushroom caps in butter. Spread toast heavily with Snail Butter. Place 4 mushroom caps on top of each piece of toast and dot with more Snail Butter. Put under the broiler for 1 or 2 minutes before serving.

Serves 6.

Snail Butter

1 cup butter, softened
3 cloves garlic, finely chopped
¾ to 1 cup finely
  chopped parsley

¼ cup finely chopped chives
  (optional)

Knead together butter, garlic and parsley. Add chives and blend well. Chill for 1 hour.

Makes about 1½ cups.

TARAMA SPREAD

¾ cup fresh bread crumbs
  Milk
½ cup tarama (salted cod roe,
    obtainable in Middle Eastern
    stores) or red caviar
¼ cup grated onion

2 tablespoons lemon juice
  Freshly ground black pepper
    to taste
  Chopped parsley
  Pumpernickel or rye bread,
    thinly sliced

Soak bread crumbs in milk and squeeze dry. Combine tarama with onion and beat with wooden spoon to break down texture. Add to this bread crumbs, lemon juice and pepper to taste. Blend well until mixture has good spreading consistency; add more bread crumbs if necessary. Chill. Serve in good-looking bowl. Sprinkle spread well with parsley and arrange sliced bread around bowl.

Makes about 1 cup.

ESCABECHE DE PESCADO

2 pounds white fish fillets
½ cup olive oil
1 large onion, thinly sliced
2 cloves garlic, chopped
2 fresh or canned chili peppers,
    chopped
½ cup wine vinegar
  Pinch ground cumin

  Salt and freshly ground
    black pepper to taste
1 medium orange
  Shredded lettuce
  Orange slices
  French dressing
  Grated orange rind
  Thinly shredded green
    pepper

Sauté fillets in oil until nicely browned. Remove to serving dish. In same pan (with additional oil if needed), cook onion, garlic and chili peppers. Add to this vinegar, cumin and salt and pepper to taste. Cool mixture; pour over fish. Squeeze juice of orange over this. Chill for 6 to 8 hours. Serve garnished with lettuce, orange slices marinated in dressing, orange rind and green pepper shreds.

Serves 6 to 8.

GRAVAD LAX

3- to 5-pound piece of salmon
  (from middle of fish)
Fresh dill
⅓ cup salt (kosher salt is best)
¼ cup sugar

1 teaspoon saltpeter (potassium
  nitrate; obtainable at
  drugstore)
Coarsely ground black pepper
Allspice
1 bay leaf, crushed

This salmon is not cooked by heat but by saltpeter and fresh dill. Cut salmon in two along backbone; remove bone. Line bottom of deep pan with dill sprigs. Rub salmon flesh with mixture of salt, sugar and saltpeter. Place one piece, skin side down, in pan. Sprinkle with pepper, allspice, bay leaf and a great deal more dill. Top with other piece of salmon, skin side up, and weight fish down well. Chill for 24 hours. Slice in fairly thin slices and serve with a mustardy French dressing. Delicious!

Serves 6 to 10.

BRIOCHES WITH SALMON BUTTER

2 pounds cold poached salmon
1 small onion, chopped
1 teaspoon chopped fresh dill
¼ cup chopped parsley
1 teaspoon salt

Juice of 1 lemon
½ cup butter, softened
50 Tiny Brioches (page 164)
Watercress

Chop salmon very fine with onion, dill, parsley, salt and lemon juice. Blend with butter. Remove tops from brioches and take out some of the crumb. Fill with salmon butter, replace tops and chill until ready to serve. Arrange brioches on tray decorated with sprays of watercress.

Makes 50 filled brioches.

SHRIMPS BEARD

2 pounds jumbo shrimp
3 cloves garlic, finely chopped
¼ cup chopped parsley
1 teaspoon dried basil

1 teaspoon dry mustard
1 teaspoon salt
½ cup olive or peanut oil
Juice of 1 lemon

Split through shell of each shrimp with kitchen shears. Remove black vein but leave shrimp intact. Place in bowl or jar with mixture of remaining ingredients; marinate for several hours. Grill over charcoal or in broiler for 4 to 5 minutes or until shells are browned and shrimp are just cooked through.

Serves 6.

JUMBO SHRIMP AND HOT DIP

2 pounds jumbo shrimp
3 cloves garlic, finely chopped
¼ cup chopped parsley
1 teaspoon basil
Juice of 1 lemon

1 teaspoon salt
1 teaspoon freshly ground
black pepper
4 tablespoons butter

Split back of each shrimp with kitchen shears and remove shell except for tail. Remove black vein. Poach shrimp in boiling salted water for 4 minutes; remove and cool. Reduce shrimp broth to about 1 cup. Mix garlic, parsley, basil, lemon, salt and pepper. Add with butter to shrimp broth. Heat to boiling point but do not let boil. Serve shrimp arranged on a plate next to the dip, kept warm on a hot plate or over one of those candle warmers.

Serves 6 to 8.

CRABMEAT LOUIS

Finely shredded greens	2 cups Mayonnaise (page 153)
2 pounds crabmeat	1 cup chili sauce
Juice of 2 lemons	2 cloves garlic, crushed
2 hard-cooked eggs, quartered	Salt and freshly ground
2 tomatoes, peeled and	black pepper to taste
cut into wedges	

Make bed of greens on large serving dish. Flavor crabmeat with lemon juice and place on greens. Arrange eggs and tomatoes around crabmeat. Cover with Louis dressing, made by combining mayonnaise, chili sauce, garlic and salt and pepper to taste.

Serves 8 to 10.

CRABMEAT BROIL

Cut 1 pound lean bacon strips in half crosswise. Divide 1 pound lump crabmeat into as many pieces as there are pieces of bacon. Wrap each crabmeat lump with a piece of bacon and secure with a wooden pick. Broil the rolls until the bacon is crisp and the crabmeat thoroughly heated. Sprinkle with chopped parsley and serve on a platter with large lemon wedges.

Makes about 40 rolls.

FRIED OYSTERS

Drain 8 pints oysters and dry them well. Dip in beaten eggs seasoned with a little freshly ground black pepper. Roll oysters in bread crumbs or cracker crumbs. Fry in deep fat at 375° for 2 minutes. Drain on absorbent paper. Serve with lemon wedges and a garnish of watercress.

Serves 6.

PATE DE CANARD

5- to 6-pound duckling
1-inch strip pork skin
1 leek
1 sprig thyme
1 stalk celery
1 bay leaf
4 cups chicken bouillon or stock
1 pound chicken livers
1 pound lean pork
6 shallots
1 clove garlic
3 sprigs fresh chervil
5 eggs

1 tablespoon flour
1½ teaspoons salt
⅛ teaspoon freshly ground
    black pepper
¾ cup Cognac
1 teaspoon bottled brown
    gravy coloring
1 can (4 ounces) pitted ripe
    olives, chopped
¼ pound larding pork,
    cut into thin strips
1 envelope unflavored gelatin
¼ cup cold water

With a very sharp knife, cut duck skin from neck to vent along center of breast. Pull back skin, using tip of knife where necessary to help cut connective tissue; reserve. Cut meat from duck bones; set aside. In large kettle, place bones, neck and giblets, reserving liver. Add pork skin, leek, thyme, celery, bay leaf and bouillon. Cover and bring to boil. Simmer for 2 hours.

Meanwhile, put duck meat, duck liver, chicken livers and pork through food grinder together with shallots, garlic and chervil. Add eggs to ground meat one at a time, pounding in well with mortar and pestle or wooden spoon in a heavy bowl. Mix together flour, salt and pepper and sprinkle into ground meat mixture. Add Cognac and gravy coloring; mix well. Add olives and mix again.

Line bottom of large oval 3-quart terrine or casserole or smaller casseroles of equivalent total size with duck skin. Carefully pour in meat-egg mixture. Top with larding pork. Bake uncovered in a 300° oven for 2½ hours for the 3-quart terrine or about 1 hour for 16-ounce casseroles.

When broth has simmered for 2 hours, remove cover and increase heat. Let broth reduce to about 1½ cups including fat; strain. Soften gelatin in cold water and add to hot broth. Stir until gelatin is dissolved. When pâté is removed from oven, pour broth into casserole. Weight pâté to keep it submerged in broth and let stand for 2 hours. Remove weight, cover casserole and chill thoroughly before serving.

Serves 30 to 40.

VEAL PATE

10 to 12 shallots or green
  onions, finely chopped
½ cup chopped parsley
1 pound bacon, cut into strips
2 pounds veal, cut into
  thin scallops and
  pounded flat

2 pounds ham or Canadian
  bacon, thinly sliced
Fresh black pepper
Salt (if necessary)
Thyme to taste
1 small bay leaf, crushed
½ cup dry white wine

Mix shallots with parsley. Line bottom and sides of a long 3-quart bread pan or pâté mold with bacon strips, reserving enough to cover the top of the pâté. Arrange layer of veal scallops on top of the bacon and sprinkle with shallot-parsley mixture. Arrange layer of ham slices, then another of veal, another sprinkling of shallot-parsley mixture and another layer of ham. To each layer of ham, add a grind of pepper, salt (taste it, you will probably find there is enough salt in the ham to season pâté), a little thyme and a little bay leaf. Repeat the layers until all ingredients are used. Add wine and cover top with remaining bacon strips. Cover and bake in a 300 to 325° oven for about 2 hours. Remove cover and weight pâté down; cool. (This makes it more compact and easier to cut and brings excess fat to top.) Chill pâté and serve in very thin slices with some of the natural jelly that forms around loaf.

Serves 30 to 40.

VEAL AND HAM PATE

1½ pounds finely ground veal
1½ pounds ground pork
2 cloves garlic, finely chopped
½ cup Cognac
1 teaspoon salt
1 teaspoon freshly ground
   black pepper
1 teaspoon basil
   Pinch rosemary

   Pinch nutmeg
2 eggs
½ pound salt pork or
   pork skin, cut into strips
1 pound smoked ham or Canadian bacon, sliced paper thin
1 cup chopped green onions
   and parsley, mixed
½ cup Cognac

Combine veal, pork, garlic, Cognac, salt, pepper, basil, rosemary, nutmeg and eggs. Line a 2½-quart casserole with the salt pork strips, reserving enough to cover the top of the pâté. Add layer of veal mixture; then layer of ham and generous sprinkling of onion-parsley mixture. Repeat the layers until casserole is filled, ending with veal mixture. Press down well and add Cognac. Cover with remaining pork strips. Cover and bake in a 325° oven for 2 to 2½ hours. Remove cover and weight pâté down; cool. Re-cover and chill before serving.

This will keep in its casserole for several weeks in the refrigerator if a layer of fat is kept on upper and any other exposed surfaces.

Serves 25 to 30.

HOMEMADE MEATBALLS

1 pound ground pork
1 pound ground beef
½ cup fresh bread crumbs
1½ teaspoons salt
½ teaspoon freshly ground
    black pepper
½ teaspoon oregano

Pinch tarragon
½ teaspoon ground allspice
½ teaspoon dry mustard
2 eggs
½ cup flour
½ cup butter
1 cup red wine or broth

Combine pork, beef, bread crumbs, salt, pepper, oregano, tarragon, allspice, mustard and eggs. Blend well and form into 1-inch balls. Sprinkle balls with flour and brown quickly in butter in a skillet. Add wine; cover and simmer for 35 minutes. Serve in chafing dish or hot casserole.

Makes about 50 meatballs.

CHICKEN LIVER ROLLS

½ pound bacon, sliced
1 pound chicken livers
4 tablespoons butter
    Salt and freshly ground
    black pepper to taste

½ cup finely chopped onion
    or shallot
¼ cup chopped parsley
36 Tiny Rolls (page 162)

Fry bacon until very crisp; drain and crumble. Sauté livers in butter until just cooked through but not well done. Salt and pepper to taste. Chop livers rather coarsely and combine with bacon, onion and parsley. Slice each roll in half, spread with chicken liver mixture and reassemble. Heat in a preheated 350° oven about 10 minutes.

Makes 36 rolls.

PIROSHKI

¼ pound pork
¼ pound pork liver
½ clove garlic
1 small onion, finely chopped
3 tablespoons butter
¾ teaspoon salt
½ teaspoon freshly ground
  black pepper
¼ teaspoon thyme

½ teaspoon poppy seeds
1 egg, beaten
¼ cup soft bread crumbs
  Pastry (your favorite
  two-crust recipe),
  well chilled
1 egg white
1 egg, slightly beaten

Grind together pork, pork liver and garlic. Sauté onion in butter. Add meat mixture and season with salt, pepper, thyme and poppy seeds. Cook over low flame for 15 minutes, stirring occasionally. Cool; work in egg and bread crumbs. Chill until ready to make into turnovers.

Roll pastry dough into rectangle and cut into small circles about 2 inches in diameter. Brush circles with egg white and place about 1 teaspoonful filling on each. Fold over and prick a hole or two in dough. Seal edges with pastry wheel or fork tines. Brush with egg. Place on a lightly greased baking sheet and bake in a preheated 400° oven until the piroshki are brown and the filling well cooked, about 15 minutes. Serve warm.

Makes about 50 turnovers.

2

SOUPS

CLARET CONSOMME WITH SALTED CREAM

4 cups consommé
½ cup claret (dry red
    Bordeaux wine)

½ cup heavy cream,
    whipped and lightly
    salted

Combine consommé and wine; heat. Garnish each serving with a dollop of whipped cream.

Serves 3.

ITALIAN EGG SOUP

3 to 4 cans (12 ounces each)
    chicken broth or 4½ to
    6 cups homemade broth
Grated onion, chopped celery or
    parsley sprigs

6 thick slices toast
6 eggs
    Grated onion
    Chopped parsley

Heat broth to boiling point and add seasoning—try a little onion, celery or parsley. Heat serving bowls and place a slice of toast in each. Carefully break an egg on top of each slice. When ready to serve, pour the hot broth over the eggs, filling the bowls. By the time the bowls reach the table, the broth will have set the eggs. Serve with bowls of grated onion and chopped parsley to sprinkle on the soup.

Serves 6.

WATERCRESS SOUP, CHINESE FASHION

6 cups chicken broth
Salt and freshly ground
  black pepper to taste
Dash soy sauce

2 large bunches watercress
4 well-set poached eggs
  Finely cut water chestnuts
  Thin strips smoked ham

Heat broth to boiling point and correct seasoning with salt, pepper and soy sauce. Trim off coarse ends and make a nest of the cress in the bottom of a hot tureen or soup bowl. Lower the eggs into the center of nest. Arrange them carefully and sprinkle with a little water chestnut and a few strips of smoked ham. Pour in boiling broth from the side of the tureen so that it runs down the side gently and the tureen fills up gradually. Serve each person an egg, some cress and broth. Serve with thin slices crisp buttered toast.

Serves 4.

LENTIL SOUP

2 cups lentils
3 quarts water
  Ham bone or lamb shank
1 onion, studded with
  2 cloves
1 tablespoon salt

1 bay leaf
1 clove garlic
4 frankfurters, thinly sliced
½ cup chopped green onion
½ cup chopped parsley
  Dairy sour cream (optional)

Soak lentils overnight in water to cover, then drain. In a deep casserole, place lentils with water, ham bone and onion. Add salt, bay leaf and garlic. Cover and bake in a 350° oven for 2 hours. Reduce heat to 250° and cook for 2 more hours or until the lentils are practically a puree. Remove the meat and chop any bits that may lurk on the bones. Just before serving, add frankfurters, chopped meat, onion and parsley. Serve with a large dollop of sour cream in each bowl.

Serves 8.

OYSTER STEW

1 pint fresh oysters or
   1 can (16 ounces) oysters,
   drained
Butter

4 cups light cream
Salt and freshly ground
   black pepper to taste
Dash Worcestershire sauce

Sauté oysters in butter until their edges curl. Place oysters in a casserole and pour cream over them. Add salt and pepper to taste, Worcestershire sauce and large dab of butter. Bake in a 350° oven until hot. Serve with additional dab of butter in each cup if desired.

Serves 4.

REAL CHICKEN SOUP

3 pounds chicken backs
   and necks
1 onion, studded with
   2 cloves
1 tablespoon salt
1 teaspoon tarragon
1 teaspoon freshly ground
   black pepper

1 sprig parsley
1 stalk celery
2 quarts water
½ cup uncooked rice, well
   washed
½ pound mushrooms, chopped
   Chopped parsley

In a large casserole, place chicken with onion, salt, tarragon, pepper, parsley and celery. Brown in a preheated 400° oven for 30 minutes and then add water. Cover and cook for 3 hours at 300°. Remove casserole from oven. Remove bits of meat from bones. Strain vegetables from stock. Return meat to broth with rice and mushrooms. Cover and continue cooking at 300° for 45 minutes. Sprinkle with parsley and serve with buttered toast.

Serves 6 to 8.

POT AU FEU

1 oxtail
1 veal knuckle
2 pounds brisket of beef
1 pound lean salt pork
1 pound shin of beef (with bone
  if desired)
6 peppercorns
1 clove garlic
2 cloves
  Few sprigs parsley
  Pinch nutmeg

Pinch thyme
12 small carrots
6 small white onions
6 leeks
12 small white turnips, peeled
  Potatoes, boiled in their
   jackets
  Coarse salt
  Sour gherkins
  Selection of mustards

In roaster or 8-quart pot, place oxtail, veal, beef brisket, salt pork and beef shin. Cover with water. Bring to a boil; reduce heat, cover and simmer gently for 2 hours. Skin off fat occasionally during cooking.

In a small cheesecloth bag, place peppercorns, garlic, cloves, parsley sprigs, nutmeg and thyme. Add to broth with carrots, onions, leeks and turnips. Cook for 1½ hours longer.

To serve, arrange vegetables and bits of meat in large bowls and pour some broth into each. Follow the soup with a platter of the sliced beef, pieces of salt pork, oxtail and potatoes. Serve with salt, gherkins and mustards.

Serves 6.

CABBAGE SOUP

1 large veal knuckle
2 pounds shin or brisket of beef
6 onions, thinly sliced
3 carrots, thinly sliced
1 clove garlic
1 tablespoon salt

1 teaspoon rosemary
2 quarts water
1 medium head cabbage, thinly shredded
1 teaspoon salt
1 can (1 pound 13 ounces) garbanzos (chick-peas)

Place veal knuckle and beef in a casserole. Add onions, carrots, garlic, salt and rosemary. Brown quickly in a preheated 450° oven. Add water; cover and bake at 300° for 2 hours. Remove the casserole and add cabbage, salt and garbanzos. Cover and bake at 300° for 1 hour more. Remove veal knuckle and serve from casserole.

Serves 8.

3
FISH AND SHELLFISH

BAKED FILLETS, POLISH STYLE

Olive oil or butter
Dry bread crumbs
4 large fish fillets
2 medium onions, sliced
  paper thin and
  sprinkled with salt

3 tablespoons chopped fresh
  dill
1 cup dairy sour cream
Chopped parsley
Chopped fresh dill

Choose a loaf tin a little larger than the fish fillets. Oil it well and sprinkle heavily with bread crumbs. Place in it, in alternate layers, fish fillets, onions, dill and a spreading of sour cream. Top with a layer of sour cream and mask the sides thickly with sour cream. Bake in a preheated 375° oven about 25 minutes or until the sour cream is a golden color.

Unmold the loaf; sprinkle with parsley and dill. The onions will not be cooked through but will flavor the fish and be of an interesting texture. This should be portioned by cutting into slices rather than by lifting off the fillets.

Serves 4.

This calls for boiled potatoes with plenty of butter, sliced tomatoes and cucumbers and toasted French bread. A hot coffee cake would be excellent for dessert.

BAKED FILLETS, PIONEER STYLE

2 medium onions, thinly sliced
4 tablespoons butter
  Salt to taste
4 white fish fillets

Freshly ground black
  pepper to taste
½ cup buttered bread crumbs
1 tablespoon chopped parsley
2 slices crisp bacon, crumbled

Sauté onions in butter until just transparent; salt to taste. Oil a shallow casserole. Arrange fish fillets in casserole and sprinkle with salt and pepper. Cover with the sautéed onions and sprinkle with bread crumbs. Bake in a preheated 400° oven until fish is cooked, 12 to 15 minutes. Sprinkle with chopped parsley and bacon. Serve at once.

Serves 4.

Serve this with tiny new potatoes or canned potatoes and peas. A lemon rice pudding would be good for dessert.

FILLET OF SOLE NETHERLANDS

2 tablespoons butter	1 tablespoon sherry
1 tablespoon water	1 tablespoon heavy cream
1½ pounds sole fillets	Salt and freshly ground
1 teaspoon lemon juice	black pepper

Blend 1 tablespoon butter with water in a skillet over low heat. Arrange fillets in skillet and sauté gently 8 to 10 minutes, turning them once. Remove the fillets to a hot shallow casserole. Add to the sauce in the hot skillet 1 more tablespoon butter, lemon juice, sherry and heavy cream. Add salt and pepper to taste. Pour the hot mixture over the fillets and brown lightly under broiler.

Serves 4.

Serve with plain boiled potatoes and a cucumber salad. A fruit tart would be a good dessert.

FLOUNDER FILLETS WITH MUSHROOMS AND ONIONS

12 small white onions
4 good-size flounder fillets
½ pound small mushrooms, sliced
2 small carrots, cut into very fine short strips

Salt and freshly ground black pepper
2 tablespoons chopped parsley
¼ to ½ teaspoon rosemary
8 thin slices lemon
⅓ cup butter
⅓ cup dry white wine

Parboil onions in salted water; drain and set aside. Arrange flounder fillets in a buttered shallow casserole. Arrange around them the onions, mushrooms and carrots. Sprinkle lightly with salt and a little more heavily with pepper. Add parsley, rosemary and lemon slices. Melt butter in wine and pour over. Bake in a preheated 325° oven until the fish flakes easily with a fork, 20 minutes.

Serves 4.

With the fish, have plain boiled potatoes with parsley butter and a heaping platter of asparagus cooked just long enough so there's a bit of crispness left. And the dessert suggestion is fruits and cheese.

GREEN PEPPERS STUFFED WITH OCEAN PERCH

2 packages (16-ounce size) frozen ocean perch fillets
6 equal-size green peppers
6 tablespoons diced bacon
3 tablespoons chopped onion
¼ cup chopped celery
¼ cup chili sauce

1 teaspoon salt
¼ teaspoon freshly ground black pepper
½ clove garlic, crushed
4 tablespoons butter, melted
1 cup dry bread crumbs
6 ripe tomatoes

Thaw perch fillets and cut into ½-inch pieces. Cut a slice from the top of each green pepper and remove seeds. Parboil them in lightly salted water for 7 minutes; drain. Fry bacon until crisp; add onion, celery, chili sauce, salt, pepper and fish. Simmer for 10 minutes, then stuff into peppers.

Let garlic stand in butter 10 minutes. Combine with bread crumbs. Spread half of this mixture over the peppers. Remove a slice from the stem end of each tomato. Top the tomatoes with the remaining buttered bread crumb mixture, pressing it in a little. Arrange the stuffed peppers and tomatoes alternately in a well-greased shallow casserole. Bake in a preheated 350° oven for 20 to 25 minutes.

Serves 6.

With a cucumber salad, French bread and sliced oranges and apples with grapes, this will give you a wonderful dinner.

OCEAN PERCH PIE

---

1 package (16 ounces) frozen ocean perch fillets	¼ teaspoon freshly ground black pepper
1 quart water	1½ cups milk
1 large onion, sliced	2 cups diced cooked potatoes
2 tablespoons butter	¾ cup grated Swiss cheese
2 tablespoons flour	Pastry (your favorite
¾ teaspoon salt	one-crust recipe)

Thaw perch fillets and place in boiling salted water. Reduce heat and simmer until fish flakes easily with a fork, 10 minutes. Drain and flake. Cook onion in butter until tender. Blend in flour, salt and pepper. When smooth, add milk gradually and cook gently until thickened, stirring constantly. Add potatoes, cheese and fish. Stir 1 to 2 minutes, then pour into a well-greased casserole.

Roll out the pie pastry and cover the casserole with it, sealing the edges and pricking the center in 2 or 3 places with a fork. Bake in a preheated 450° oven until browned, about 20 minutes.

Serves 6.

You might complement this with a crisp mélange of greens, raw mushrooms, croutons and a bacon-vinegar dressing. Try pancakes with jelly for dessert or waffles with currant jelly and grated orange rind.

FISH PUDDING

½ cup butter
½ cup flour
2 cups milk

Salt and freshly ground
  black pepper to taste
3 eggs, well beaten
1 pound cod, boiled and flaked

Melt butter in the top of a double boiler. Blend in flour; add milk and salt and pepper to taste. Stir until smooth. Then beat in eggs and fold in boiled flaked cod. Pour all this mixture into a well-greased casserole and bake in a preheated 350° oven for 45 minutes or until just firm.

Serves 4.

New potatoes with plenty of butter and parsley and chives are a must with this. And serve a crisp cucumber salad and hot rolls. Have old-fashioned apple betty for dessert.

CREOLE HALIBUT

2-pound halibut steak
2 tablespoons butter
  Salt and freshly ground
    black pepper

½ cup water
1 cup Creole Sauce (page 160)

Sear halibut steak in a greased shallow casserole in a preheated 450° oven for 10 minutes. Reduce heat to 325°; dot halibut with butter and sprinkle lightly with salt and pepper. Add water to casserole and cook for 20 minutes. Cover with sauce and cook 5 minutes more.

Serves 4.

This calls for rice, which may be baked in the oven along with the fish. And why not continue the pepper flavor with sautéed green pepper strips sprinkled with a little bit of nutmeg? For dessert, a Nesselrode pie would be elegant.

FINNAN HADDIE DELMONICO

1 pound boneless finnan haddie
4 tablespoons butter
4 tablespoons flour
1½ cups light cream
Freshly ground black pepper

Paprika
Salt
½ cup grated cheese
Buttered bread crumbs
Grated cheese

Cover fish with boiling water and simmer for 10 minutes on low heat. Drain and flake the fish.

Melt the butter and blend in the flour. Add the cream, stirring constantly. Season to taste with pepper, paprika and salt (if the fish is not too salty). Continue stirring and cooking until the sauce is thickened.

Combine the sauce with the flaked fish and grated cheese. Pour into a buttered casserole. Top with bread crumbs and additional cheese. Bake in a preheated 375° oven for 20 to 25 minutes or until the top is brown and crusty.

Serves 4.

Serve with toasted protein bread and a mixture of sliced cucumbers and onions with a vinegary dressing. Dessert is baked pears with heavy cream.

HADDOCK WITH OYSTERS

---

2 haddock fillets
   (about 8 ounces each)
½ teaspoon salt
½ teaspoon freshly ground
   black pepper

½ pint oysters,
   washed and cleaned
1 cup cracker crumbs
   Juice of 1 lemon
¼ cup butter

Place 1 haddock fillet in a greased casserole and sprinkle with salt and pepper. Dip oysters in cracker crumbs and cover the fillet with them. Place remaining fillet on top of the oysters. Fasten in place with wooden picks. Sprinkle with more crumbs and the lemon juice; dot with butter. Bake in a preheated 350° oven for 30 minutes.

Serves 4.

This delicacy might be preceded by some vichyssoise. Have shoestring potatoes with the fish, and zucchini with garlic and olive oil. For dessert, serve brownies and ice cream.

DEVILED TUNA

---

2 cups flaked tuna fish
2 tablespoons chopped parsley
2 teaspoons lemon juice
2 teaspoons prepared mustard
½ teaspoon drained prepared
   horseradish

2 hard-cooked eggs, chopped
   Salt and freshly ground
   black pepper to taste
1½ cups thick Béchamel Sauce
   (page 156)
   Buttered bread crumbs

Combine all ingredients except for bread crumbs. Pour into a well-greased casserole and top with the crumbs. Bake in a preheated 350° oven until brown, about 15 minutes.

Serves 4.

A rice pilaf and chopped spinach go well with this tuna dish. You might serve an orange and onion salad too. If you still want dessert, ice cream would be pleasant.

TRUCK GARDEN SALMON

2½ pounds salmon steaks or fillets
   Salt and freshly ground black pepper
1 cup cooked fresh or canned whole-kernel corn
1½ cups cooked cut-up green beans

2 cups sliced boiled potatoes
¼ cup melted butter
2 tablespoons lemon juice
2 tablespoons grated onion
2 tablespoons chopped parsley
2 tomatoes, peeled and sliced
   Grated Parmesan cheese

Cut fish into serving portions and sprinkle with a little salt and pepper. Arrange layers of corn, beans and potatoes in a well-greased casserole, sprinkling each layer lightly with salt and pepper.

Combine melted butter with lemon juice, onion and parsley. Dip the salmon into this mixture and place on top of the potatoes. Now cover all with the tomato slices. Pour on any remaining butter mixture and top generously with grated Parmesan. Bake in a preheated 350° oven for 1¼ hours.

Serves 6.

With this, no side dish is needed but a cucumber salad. For dessert, you might bake an apple charlotte at the same time the salmon is in the oven.

SALMON BAKED IN SOUR CREAM WITH DILL

1½-pound salmon fillet
Salt and freshly ground
  black pepper
6 medium potatoes, peeled
  Butter
1½ cups dairy sour cream

⅓ teaspoon celery salt
1 tablespoon grated onion
1 tablespoon chopped fresh dill
1 lemon, sliced paper thin
  Paprika

Remove the skin from salmon fillet. Sprinkle the fillet with salt and a little freshly ground black pepper. Lay it in a well-greased shallow casserole. Cut potatoes with a ball cutter, rub the balls thoroughly with butter and place around fish.

Now combine sour cream with celery salt, onion and dill. Spread over the salmon and potatoes. Garnish with lemon slices sprinkled with a little paprika. Bake 30 to 35 minutes in a preheated 350° oven.

Serves 4 to 6.

A cucumber and onion salad is a must with this, as is crisp French bread and butter.

SEAFOOD CHOWDER

½ cup finely chopped onion
2 tablespoons butter
1 cup finely diced potatoes
  Clam, oyster or any
    fish liquid
1½ quarts milk
  Salt and freshly ground
    black pepper to taste
½ teaspoon thyme

  Paprika
½ pint oysters
½ pint clams
½ pint scallops
½ pound crabmeat
½ pound shelled shrimp
¼ cup butter
¼ cup Cognac
  Chopped parsley

Sauté onion in butter until just wilted and clear. Add potatoes and cover with fish liquid. Simmer until potatoes are tender. If there isn't enough fish liquid to cover potatoes, add water to cover. Combine with milk and heat to the boiling point. Season with salt and pepper, thyme and a dash paprika. Just before serving, add oysters, clams, scallops, crabmeat and shrimp. Cook together for 4 minutes. Add butter and Cognac. Serve in bowls with chopped parsley and paprika.

Serves 6.

Toasted French or Italian bread is my choice to serve with this chowder, though tradition calls for pilot crackers. Poached pears with ginger make a refreshing dessert.

DEVILED OYSTERS

---

36 oysters (in the shell)	Cayenne pepper
2 tablespoons minced onion	1 egg, beaten
2 tablespoons butter	1 teaspoon prepared mustard
3 tablespoons flour	1 tablespoon Worcestershire
1½ cups milk	sauce
1 teaspoon salt	2 tablespoons chopped parsley
¼ teaspoon nutmeg	Buttered bread crumbs

Shuck oysters; reserve the deep halves of the shell. Chop the meat. Sauté onion in butter until tender. Blend in flour. When smooth, add milk, salt, nutmeg and a few grains cayenne. Cook gently, stirring constantly, until thickened.

Add a few tablespoons of the sauce to egg. Return egg mixture to sauce with the oysters, mustard, Worcestershire and parsley. Blend and fill the shells. Place in a baking dish and top each with bread crumbs. Bake 10 minutes or until browned in a preheated 400° oven.

Serves 6.

Serve corn bread with this, and a fruit dessert like flambéed peaches.

CHINESE SHRIMPS WITH PINEAPPLE

3 green onions, finely shredded
4 tablespoons peanut oil
5 water chestnuts, finely sliced
1 cup canned pineapple chunks
½ cup pineapple juice
1 tablespoon vinegar
¼ cup finely shredded green pepper

¼ cup Chinese pickles
1 tablespoon grated or cut preserved ginger
1 tablespoon cornstarch, mixed with a little water
1 pound shrimp, shelled

Prepare a sauce by sautéeing onions lightly in oil, adding the next 7 ingredients and thickening with cornstarch. Bring sauce to a boil. Add shrimp and cook gently in sauce for 4 minutes. If the sauce is too thick, add a little more pineapple juice.

Serves 4.

Boiled rice is a must with this. A coffee soufflé would make a pleasant ending to the meal.

ROCK LOBSTER DIVINE

2 frozen or thawed South African rock lobster tails (about 8 ounces each)
1 package (12 ounces) frozen asparagus tips
4 tablespoons flour

4 tablespoons butter
2 cups milk
Salt and freshly ground black pepper to taste
1 tablespoon prepared mustard
1 cup grated Cheddar cheese

Place lobster tails in a kettle of boiling lightly salted water. When the water comes back to a boil, lower heat and cook, covered, for 1 minute longer than the lobsters' weight. (Cook an 8-ounce tail 9 minutes.) Drain, then remove the meat. Dice or leave in chunks.

Cook asparagus tips until just barely tender. Prepare a cream sauce with flour, butter and milk. Season with salt and pepper to taste. Blend in mustard and cheese; stir until well blended. Arrange the asparagus in a shallow casserole. Place lobster meat on top and pour sauce evenly over all. Bake in a preheated 450° oven until sauce is bubbly, about 10 minutes.

Serves 4.

This is excellent served with heated potato chips and some watercress. You might also have a crisp-crusted apple pie with cream for dessert, along with plenty of coffee.

LOBSTER AU GRATIN

2 cups diced cooked or canned
    lobster meat
2 tablespoons butter
    Salt
    Tabasco sauce
1 tablespoon sherry

1 tablespoon Cognac
½ cup heavy cream
2 to 3 tablespoons grated
    Parmesan cheese
    Buttered bread crumbs

Sauté lobster meat in butter for several minutes. Pour into a shallow casserole with a little salt and a dash of Tabasco sauce. Add sherry, Cognac and heavy cream blended with cheese. Sprinkle with buttered crumbs and more cheese and brown in a preheated 375° oven for 20 minutes.

Serves 4.

With this serve noodles with butter, a cucumber salad and some chocolate tarts.

SHREVEPORT CRABMEAT

2 tablespoons butter	½ cup light cream
2 cups crabmeat	2 egg yolks, well beaten
Salt and freshly ground	½ cup grated cheese
black pepper to taste	Lemon wedges

Melt butter in top of double boiler; add crabmeat and salt and pepper to taste. Cook for 5 minutes over hot water. Mix cream with egg yolks and add to the hot crabmeat. Cook this 4 minutes over low heat, stirring constantly. Pour into a casserole and sprinkle cheese over the top. Bake in a preheated 350° oven until cheese is melted, about 15 minutes. Serve with lemon wedges.

Serves 4.

Serve this with French-fried potatoes or heated potato chips and a cauliflower coleslaw with slivers of green pepper.

'4
MEATS

HUNGARIAN POT ROAST

4- to 6-pound pot roast,
  larded with ¼-inch strips
  salt pork
4 tablespoons butter or
  olive oil
1 teaspoon salt

2½ teaspoons Hungarian
  paprika
¼ teaspoon nutmeg
½ cup beef stock or bouillon
1 cup dairy sour cream

Sear pot roast well in butter. Place in a deep casserole or Dutch oven with salt, 1½ teaspoons paprika, nutmeg and stock. Cover and cook 25 minutes to the pound in a 325° oven, adding more liquid if needed. When done, skim excess fat from sauce. Add remaining paprika and sour cream. Blend thoroughly.

Serves 6 to 8.

Buttered noodles generously sprinkled with parsley are a must with this, as are sautéed mushrooms. And this might be a good time for an easy dessert that you'll never forget: Make a pile of thin, thin pancakes; put scrapings of sweet chocolate between each one as you pile them up; cut in wedges, like cake, and serve with whipped cream.

BOEUF EN DAUBE AU VIN BLANC

1 large onion, finely chopped
1 large carrot, finely chopped
½ pound smoked ham,
   finely chopped
   3-pound beef round roast
   (top or bottom)
1 calf's foot

3 cups dry white wine
1 cup water
1 cup beef stock
  Salt to taste
1 bay leaf
  Peppercorns

Spread onion, carrot and ham over the bottom of a deep casserole. Place on this the roast and calf's foot. Add wine, water and stock. Cover and cook in a 250 to 275° oven for 2 hours. Turn meat and add more liquid in original proportion to bring amount in casserole to about 4 cups. Season with salt to taste, bay leaf and a few peppercorns. Cover and cook 2 hours longer.

Remove meat and calf's foot. Strain and reserve stock; there should be several cups left. Return meat to casserole and set aside. When the stock cools, skim off any fat; pour the clear liquid back over meat and let chill until set. (As the whole object of this dish is to have the clear jelly around the meat, the deeper and narrower your casserole is, the better the final results will be.) Serve meat cold in its own jelly.

Serves 6 to 8.

Potato salad (hot or cold) and marinated cooked vegetables go well with this dish. A fruit cobbler, warm from the oven, makes a good finish.

BRAISED BEEF BOURGEOISE

5-pound rolled boned beef
  chuck roast, larded well
  with bacon strips
Salt
Freshly ground black pepper
Nutmeg
2 cups dry red wine

½ cup brandy
3 tablespoons butter
12 medium onions
6 white turnips, halved
2 small calf's feet
4 carrots, sliced

Rub the meat well with salt, pepper and nutmeg. Place in a good-size bowl; pour in wine and brandy. Let meat marinate 6 hours, turning occasionally.

Meanwhile, melt the butter in a large skillet. Add the onions and turnips and sauté until they are lightly glazed. Set aside.

Place beef and calf's feet in heavy pot with marinade. Cover and simmer over very low heat for 1¾ hours or until the meat is nearly tender. Remove the beef to a casserole. Cut meat from calf's feet and add to beef. Add carrots and glazed onions and turnips. Strain the liquid in which the meat was cooked back over the meat. Cover and bake in a preheated 325° oven for 45 minutes or until meat is tender and vegetables are done. Add more wine if necessary. Serve hot. Cover any leftover meat with the strained braising liquid and chill until jelled; serve cold.

Serves 6 to 8.

Hot French bread and a big green salad are good accompaniments for either hot or cold braised beef. Serve a dry red wine throughout the meal and fruit and cheese for dessert.

CHURRASCO

7-pound sirloin steak,
about 3 inches thick, or
2 steaks with a combined
weight of 7 pounds or more
½ cup butter, melted
Dried rosemary
2 cups finely chopped
green onion

2 cups butter
1½ teaspoons salt
1 tablespoon freshly ground
black pepper
1 cup white wine
½ cup wine vinegar

This South American version of beefsteak is wonderfully good eating. Broil the steak over charcoal. During the cooking baste once or twice with melted butter seasoned to taste with rosemary. Cook the meat just to the rare state and char it at the last minute.

Meanwhile prepare the following sauce: Sauté onion in 1 cup butter until just soft. Add a dash or two of rosemary, then the salt, pepper, wine and vinegar. Bring this to a boil, lower the heat and simmer for 5 minutes. Taste for seasoning and add the remaining cup of butter.

When the steak is ready, cut it in rather thin diagonal slices and put them in the sauce for a minute. Serve each person some of the sauce with the meat.

Serves 6.

Good accompaniments for this dish are home-fried potatoes, sautéed or roasted onions and French bread.

ZRAZYS NELSON

5 potatoes, boiled
Butter
Salt and freshly ground
black pepper to taste
2 small cucumbers, peeled and
thinly sliced

8 mushrooms, thinly sliced
2 tablespoons flour
1 cup light cream
1 tablespoon tomato puree
8 medallions of beef
(fillet or sirloin)

Peel potatoes and cut into even rounds. Sauté in butter until nicely browned and crisp on the edges. Season to taste with salt and pepper and arrange on a hot serving platter.

Sauté cucumbers and mushrooms in butter until cucumbers are soft and mushrooms slightly browned. Add flour and mix well. Slowly pour in cream, stirring constantly. Continue stirring until thickened. Blend in tomato puree; season to taste with salt and pepper. Put aside to keep warm.

Now sauté the beef in extra butter. When done, place on the potatoes and cover with sauce.

Serves 8.

For an elegant dinner party, you might start with smoked salmon or a clear soup. Accompany the meat with French-fried onions. After the main course have salad and a cheese board, strawberry roll for dessert and then coffee and Cognac.

BEEF ROLLS ST. EMILION

3 tablespoons beef or goose fat
   or butter
½ pound mushrooms,
   coarsely chopped
½ pound smoked ham,
   coarsely chopped
1 clove garlic, finely chopped
2 tablespoons chopped parsley
4 tablespoons bread crumbs
   Salt and freshly ground
   black pepper to taste
6 to 8 large pieces beef round
   steak, each about ½ inch
   thick and 4 x 6 inches
   Butter or beef fat

2 medium onions, finely cut
2 medium carrots, finely cut
1 teaspoon thyme
2 or 3 cloves
   Piece of bay leaf
   Few celery leaves
4 tablespoons butter
½ cup white wine
½ cup beef bouillon
6 to 8 boiled potatoes
¼ cup minced parsley
12 to 16 small white onions,
   sautéed and glazed in
   butter and 1 teaspoon sugar

Prepare a stuffing by melting fat in a skillet. Sauté mushrooms and ham until nicely blended. Add garlic, parsley and bread crumbs. Blend together for 2 minutes and add salt and pepper to taste. Place several spoonfuls of this mixture on each piece of beef; roll and tie securely with a string.

Coat the inside of a casserole or heavy skillet with butter. Cover with a layer of onions and carrots. Add thyme, cloves, bay leaf and celery leaves. Heat butter in another skillet. Brown the beef rolls very quickly, then lay them on the bed of chopped vegetables. Sprinkle with salt and pepper to taste. Cover and heat until the vegetables are steaming, about 10 minutes. Add wine and bouillon. Continue cooking very slowly on top of the stove or in a 300° oven for 1½ to 2 hours or until tender. Remove rolls to a hot platter and remove the strings. Reduce the sauce over a brisk fire and taste for seasoning. Pour over the rolls.

Surround with boiled potatoes. Sprinkle with parsley. Decorate platter with glazed onions.

Serves 6 to 8.

I like salad and cheese served as a separate course after the beef rolls. A wine jelly makes an attractive ending to the meal.

SESAME RIBS

6 pounds beef short ribs, cut into individual serving portions
Seasoned flour
1 egg, beaten
2 cups sesame seeds
½ cup butter
1 cup tomato puree
2 tablespoons chili powder
4 cloves garlic, crushed or finely chopped
2 tablespoons chopped parsley
1 teaspoon cumin seed
½ teaspoon coriander (or 1 tablespoon chopped fresh coriander leaves [*cilantro*] if possible)
2 fresh or canned hot chili peppers, chopped
½ cup beef broth
½ cup pitted ripe olives, whole or sliced
½ cup blanched almonds

Dredge ribs in seasoned flour, dip in egg and then roll in sesame seeds until thoroughly coated. Brown quickly in butter and transfer to a casserole. Add tomato puree, chili powder, garlic, parsley, cumin seed, coriander and chili peppers. Add broth, cover and bake 2 hours in a 300° oven, basting frequently and adding a little more broth if needed. Add olives and almonds. Cook 15 minutes longer or until the meat is tender.

Serves 4 to 6.

If you're feeling adventurous, serve with polenta or tortillas. A cooling coleslaw wouldn't be amiss, and if you like beer, here's a good spot for it. For dessert, have cream cheese and guava jelly with some crackers.

BEEF CASSEROLE WITH OLIVES

12 small white onions
3 tablespoons beef fat
   or butter
2½ pounds beef chuck,
   cut into good-size cubes
   Flour

Salt and freshly ground
   black pepper
1 teaspoon rosemary
1 cup beef stock or bouillon
1 cup green olives (the small
   Italian or Spanish are best)
¼ cup chopped parsley

Brown onions very lightly in fat. Dredge beef well in flour seasoned with salt and pepper. Brown quickly and transfer with the onions to a casserole. Add ½ teaspoon pepper and the rosemary. Pour stock over meat, cover and bake 1 hour in a 350° oven. Add olives and parsley. Continue cooking, covered, for 30 minutes or until meat is nice and tender.

Serves 4 to 6.

Variation

Beef Casserole Niçoise: Substitute 1 cup tomato puree and ½ cup tomato juice for the stock. Add 2 cloves garlic, minced, and substitute ripe olives for the green.

This dish, in either version, really calls for liquid accompaniment. Either a good red wine or a bottle of beer is delicious! And for the meal itself, serve the meat with braised cabbage, boiled small new potatoes and a selection of pickles.

BASIC OLD-FASHIONED MEAT LOAF

1 pound ground beef	2 eggs, beaten
1 pound ground pork	½ cup fresh bread crumbs,
1 pound ground veal	soaked in beef bouillon and
½ cup chopped green onions	squeezed dry
½ cup chopped parsley	½ teaspoon rosemary
1 teaspoon salt	Dash nutmeg
1½ teaspoons freshly ground	Bacon strips, pork skins or
black pepper	salt pork strips

Combine beef, pork and veal with onions, parsley, salt, pepper, eggs, bread crumbs, rosemary and nutmeg. Mix thoroughly with hands and shape into a loaf. Place a layer of bacon strips on the bottom of an earthenware baking dish or casserole and place the loaf on the strips. Top with a few bacon strips. Bake uncovered in a 325° oven for 1½ to 2 hours, basting occasionally with the pan juices. This is delicious hot but much better—to my taste buds—weighted down and served cold.

Serves 6 to 8.

Variations

Meat Loaf Bouquetière: Prepare and shape meat mixture as above. Place in large casserole or baking dish, top with carrot strips and surround with whole baby carrots and small white onions. Bake in a 325° oven for 45 minutes. Add small whole potatoes and small whole turnips that have been parboiled for 10 minutes. Baste with pan juices and continue baking until meat is thoroughly done, 45 minutes longer.

Italian Meat Loaf: Add 3 cloves garlic, finely chopped, 1 cup whole pitted ripe olives, ½ cup tomato puree and 1 teaspoon chopped fresh basil (omit the rosemary) to the meat mixture. Cover loaf with a thin layer of tomato puree and top with bacon or salt pork strips. Bake as above.

French Meat Loaf: Substitute 1 pound chopped beef liver for the ground beef in basic recipe. Add 1 cup red wine to pan. Bake as above, basting frequently with wine and pan juices.

California Meat Loaf: Add 2 cloves garlic, finely chopped, and 1 cup pimiento-stuffed green olives to basic loaf. Add ½ cup orange juice and juice of 2 lemons to pan. Bake as above, basting frequently.

Indian Meat Loaf: Add 2 cloves garlic, finely chopped, 2 green peppers, chopped, ½ cup tomato puree and 1½ tablespoons curry powder to basic mixture. Bake as above, basting with 1 cup pineapple juice mixed with 1 teaspoon curry powder.

Mexican Meat Loaf: Add 1 tablespoon chili powder, a pinch cumin, ½ cup pine nuts and 3 small green peppers, finely chopped, to basic mixture. Bake as above, basting with a combination of ½ cup tomato puree, ½ cup tomato juice, 3 cloves garlic, finely chopped, and 1 tablespoon chili powder.

Hot, any of these loaves is elegant with rice or mashed potatoes or crisp fried ones. Broiled or baked tomatoes should go along too. Cold, serve with a rice salad or a potato salad and perhaps hot asparagus with hollandaise sauce. Try melon for dessert.

BEEF AND VEGETABLE LOAF

2 pounds finely ground beef	½ cup chopped parsley
½ pound ground salt pork	3 eggs, beaten
½ cup soft bread crumbs	1 teaspoon salt
1 large onion, finely grated	1 teaspoon dry mustard
1 large carrot, finely grated	2 tablespoons chili sauce
1 green pepper, finely grated	¼ to ½ pound bacon strips
2 cloves garlic, finely chopped	Onion rings
½ cup chopped green onions	Thinly sliced carrot

Combine ground beef, salt pork, bread crumbs, onion, carrot, green pepper, garlic, green onions, parsley, eggs, salt, mustard and chili sauce. Blend well together and form into a loaf. Place on top of bacon strips in a casserole. Top with onion rings, sliced carrot and more bacon strips. Cover and bake for 1 hour in a preheated 325° oven. Uncover and continue baking for 35 to 45 minutes, basting frequently.

Serves 4 to 6.

This is amazingly good with marble-size potatoes browned in butter until crisp. Serve with them a romaine salad dressed with lemon juice and olive oil. Have a good pumpkin pie for dessert.

BEEFSTEAK BISMARCK

2 pounds ground beef
2 tablespoons melted butter
½ cup finely chopped
   green onions

1 teaspoon salt
2 teaspoons freshly ground
   black pepper
4 soft fried eggs

Mix together ground beef, melted butter, green onions, salt and pepper. Form into 4 cakes and broil until done to taste. Serve each hamburger cake topped with a hot fried egg.

Serves 4.

For accompaniments have plain boiled potatoes liberally dressed with butter and chopped parsley, tomatoes broiled with a seasoning of finely chopped garlic and basil and plenty of cold ale. Homemade cheesecake would be nice for dessert.

ROMAN HAMBURGERS

8 thin slices eggplant
   Flour
   Salt and freshly ground
      black pepper

1 pound ground beef
1 small onion, grated
1 small clove garlic, grated
   Barbecue or tomato sauce

Dredge eggplant in flour seasoned with salt and pepper. Grill lightly just until slices are brown and tender; keep them hot. To the ground beef add onion and garlic. Season to taste with salt and pepper. Form into 4 patties about the size of the eggplant slices. Broil or pan-broil quickly. Serve each hamburger patty sandwiched between 2 eggplant slices, with your favorite sauce poured over each serving.

Serves 4.

Buttered noodles and a mixed green salad are good accompaniments. Apple crunch makes a pleasant dessert.

MEATBALLS AND PASTA

2 tablespoons olive or
   peanut oil
1½ cups finely chopped onions
1 green pepper, finely chopped
1 can (4 ounces) sliced
   mushrooms, drained
1 cup canned tomatoes
   (preferably the Italian
   plum variety)
1 pound ground beef

Salt and freshly ground
   black pepper to taste
Basil
2 tablespoons butter
1 pound noodles, spaghetti or
   macaroni, cooked and
   drained
Grated Parmesan or
   Romano cheese

This is a simple approach to a famous recipe that takes days of preparation.

Heat the oil in a skillet and add onions, green pepper and mushrooms. Cook for 7 to 8 minutes. Add tomatoes and simmer while you prepare the meat. Season beef with salt, pepper and basil and form into tiny meatballs. Melt the butter in a skillet and add the meatballs, rolling the pan around to make sure that the meat browns on all sides.

In the bottom of a greased casserole, arrange a layer of a third of the pasta and cover with half the meatballs. Add another layer of half the remaining pasta, then the rest of the meatballs. Top with the remaining pasta and pour the tomato sauce over all. Sprinkle with grated cheese. Cover and bake in a preheated 375° oven for 30 minutes. Remove the cover for the last 10 minutes and sprinkle with a little more cheese.

Serves 4 to 6.

Serve this with a salad of tomatoes and romaine tossed with a good garlicky dressing. A bottle of red wine, bread and cheese complete this dinner to perfection.

BEEF AND GINGER FRIED RICE

8 green onions, finely shredded
4 tablespoons peanut oil
¼ cup chopped fresh or
  preserved red ginger
4 to 6 dried Chinese
  mushrooms, soaked in a
  little water
1 cup shredded beef

Chopped parsley or Chinese
  parsley (also known as fresh
  coriander or *cilantro*)
3 cups cooked rice
Soy sauce
2 eggs, well beaten
Shredded green onion
Shredded ham

Sauté green onions in oil over high heat for 1 minute. Add ginger, mushrooms, beef and a little parsley. Sauté for 5 minutes, add rice and blend well. Season with a little soy sauce. Just before removing from the fire, stir in eggs and toss thoroughly. Serve with a garnish of green onion and ham.

Serves 4.

Have a tossed green salad with this, carrying out the Chinese theme by adding a little soy sauce to the salad dressing. Banana pudding makes a pleasant finale to the meal.

DEVILED BEEF BONES

---

3 or 4 leftover bones of a beef
    rib roast (leave plenty of
    meat on them when you
    carve them away from
    the roast)

2 tablespoons tarragon
    vinegar
½ cup butter, melted
    Sifted dry bread crumbs
    Sauce Diable (page 158)

This is a fine way to use the bones of a rib roast if you can withhold them from the begging crowd. Separate the ribs and dip in mixture of vinegar and half the melted butter. Roll in bread crumbs to coat. Bake in a preheated 425° oven for 25 minutes, then brush with remaining melted butter. Broil for 10 to 20 minutes, turning occasionally; the crumbs should be brown. Serve with Sauce Diable.

Serves 2.

Serve with sautéed potatoes and a tomato and onion salad. Fruit and cheese make a nice ending to the meal.

QUICK AND EASY BEEFSTEAK PIE

---

2 medium onions, sliced
3 tablespoons butter
½ teaspoon salt
½ cup chili sauce
1 can (10 ounces) beef gravy

½ pound mushrooms, sliced
    and sautéed (optional)
2 cups diced leftover beef
2 cups biscuit mix
⅓ cup chopped parsley

Sauté onions in butter until just soft. Combine with salt, chili sauce, gravy and mushrooms. Blend well with the beef and spoon into a 1½-quart casserole. Prepare biscuit mix according to package directions, adding the parsley. Top casserole with this. Bake in a preheated 425° oven for 15 minutes. Reduce heat to 350° and bake 5 to 6 minutes more or until biscuit topping is cooked through and browned.

Serves 4.

Serve with coleslaw, and for dessert, thawed frozen raspberries and peaches.

HEARTY OXTAIL RAGOUT

3 to 4 pounds oxtails,
   cut into sections
2 or 3 pig's feet, cut in half
2 onions, each studded with
   2 cloves
2 teaspoons salt
1 teaspoon freshly ground
   black pepper
3 large onions, thinly sliced
3 carrots, sliced

6 leeks, cut in half
   lengthwise
1 teaspoon thyme
1 teaspoon rosemary
1 bay leaf
1 teaspoon powdered ginger
1½ cups dry red wine
   Flour
   Butter

Place oxtails, pig's feet and onions in casserole. Add salt and pepper. Brown quickly in a preheated 450° oven (this will take approximately 30 minutes).

Add to the casserole the sliced onions, carrots, leeks, thyme, rosemary, bay leaf, ginger, wine and enough water to cover. Cover and bake for 4 to 5 hours.

Pour off the juices into a saucepan and place over low heat. Mash together equal quantities of flour and butter with a fork. Form into small balls. Stir these gradually into the juices, cooking until slightly thickened. Return the juices to the casserole. Serve with potatoes cooked in their jackets and some sour pickles.

Serves 4.

Coleslaw is a good accompaniment to this substantial dish. A light dessert like lemon ice would be a suitable finale.

VITELLO TONNATO

3-pound boned and
rolled veal leg roast
(reserve the bones)
Salt and freshly ground
black pepper to taste
1 onion, sliced
Rosemary
1½ cups dry vermouth
1 envelope gelatin (if needed)

1 can (7 ounces) tuna fish
in olive oil
1 cup Mayonnaise (page 153)
1 teaspoon anchovy paste
1 clove garlic, crushed
Anchovy fillets
Thin slices pimiento
Mayonnaise (page 153)
flavored with tuna and
anchovy paste

Roast veal in a preheated 325° oven with salt, pepper, onion and a little rosemary. Baste occasionally with vermouth. Allow 25 minutes per pound of meat. Let cool.

While roast is cooking, prepare a little broth with the reserved bones and about 1 quart of water. When the veal is done, add the pan juices to the broth. Strain, then let reduce to about 1 cup over a rather brisk flame. Chill.

When roast is cool, remove strings and any surface fat. Slice meat fairly thin and arrange attractively on a platter, overlapping the slices.

The broth should have jellied by this time. If it hasn't, soak the gelatin in water 10 minutes. Add to reheated broth. Chill.

Meanwhile, flake the tuna, mashing it well with the olive oil from the can. Combine with mayonnaise, anchovy paste and garlic. Beat in some of the jellied broth. Spread this mixture lavishly over the veal slices and return to refrigerator. Just before serving, decorate the platter with anchovy fillets and pimiento. Serve with flavored mayonnaise. This is a delicious French-Italian dish for summer gastronomic delight.

Serves 4 to 6.

A mixed green salad and a cold marinated vegetable, such as zucchini, go well with this. Hot French or Italian bread and a good bottle of rosé wine make cheese and fruit a logical and delicious conclusion to the meal.

VEAL ROAST IN CASSEROLE

4- to 5-pound veal roast, larded	1 carrot, scraped and quartered
Seasoned flour	1 cup water
6 tablespoons butter	16 to 20 small white onions
1 bay leaf	16 to 20 medium-size mushroom caps
¼ teaspoon thyme	½ cup dairy sour cream
½ clove garlic, minced	1 tablespoon chopped chives

Dredge veal well in seasoned flour and brown it quickly in 4 tablespoons butter. Place it in a deep casserole with bay leaf, thyme, garlic and carrot. Add water and 2 tablespoons butter. Cover and cook 1 hour in a 300° oven, basting frequently. Uncover and remove carrot and bay leaf. Add onions and more water if necessary. Cook another 30 minutes and add mushroom caps. Cook uncovered until meat is tender, 30 minutes longer. Stir sour cream and chives into the pan juices and serve.

Serves 4 to 6.

Noodles and an endive salad are excellent with this particular veal dish. For dessert, make a white cake and serve it with sliced bananas and whipped cream.

VEAL STEW WITH VEGETABLES

3-pound veal shank	1 cup diced carrots
4 cups water	2 cups chopped peeled
1 medium onion, sliced	tomatoes
or quartered	2 cups diced potatoes
10 peppercorns	Salt and freshly ground
2 teaspoons salt	black pepper to taste
¼ teaspoon celery salt	1 tablespoon chopped parsley
1 bay leaf	1 tablespoon chopped chives
Seasoned flour	Grated Parmesan cheese
¼ cup butter or olive oil	

Have your butcher cut the meat from the shank bone, crack the bone and cut the meat into 1½-inch cubes. Place the bone, water, onion, peppercorns, salt, celery salt and bay leaf in a saucepan. Simmer, covered, for about 1¼ hours.

Dredge the meat in seasoned flour and brown it well in butter. Remove to a casserole. In the remaining fat sauté the carrots and tomatoes lightly. Add to the meat with the strained broth. Cover and bake for 40 minutes in a preheated 350° oven.

Add potatoes, salt and pepper. Cover and bake 30 minutes longer. When the vegetables are tender, stir in parsley and chives. Sprinkle generously with grated Parmesan just before serving.

Serves 4.

This casserole needs only a tossed green salad and some crisp, hot Italian bread. Pineapple crepes would be an interesting dessert.

VEAL SURPRISE

2 pounds veal shoulder or leg, cut into 2-inch cubes
Flour
2 tablespoons butter
¼ cup olive oil
1 clove garlic, crushed
1 cup tomato puree
1 cup consommé
½ bay leaf
¼ teaspoon thyme
½ teaspoon marjoram

Salt and freshly ground black pepper to taste
12 small white onions, lightly sautéed in 2 tablespoons butter
¼ pound sliced fresh mushrooms
1 cup pitted ripe olives, sliced or whole
1 teaspoon chili powder
2 chorizos (Spanish sausages), sliced

Dredge veal well in flour and brown quickly in butter and oil with garlic. Place in a deep casserole and add tomato puree, consommé, bay leaf, thyme, marjoram and salt and pepper to taste. Bake 1 hour in preheated 350° oven.

Add onions, mushrooms, olives, chili powder and chorizos. Bake 30 minutes longer and rectify the seasoning.

Serves 4 to 6.

Serve with fluffy rice, endive and celery stalks and hot rolls. For dessert, try fresh pineapple.

VEAL AND NOODLES

1 pound noodles
1 pound small white onions
1 can (10½ ounces) condensed chicken broth
1 cup dry white wine
3 pounds very thin veal scallops
Flour
Dry mustard
Thyme
Marjoram
Salt and freshly ground black pepper
4 tablespoons fat
3 tablespoons grated lemon rind
1 package (12 ounces) frozen peas, thawed
6 tablespoons butter
6 tablespoons flour
2 cups milk
Sliced pitted ripe olives

Cook noodles in boiling salted water about 9 minutes until tender, not mushy. Boil onions until tender in chicken broth and wine. Skim out onions, reserving broth. Dredge veal well in flour seasoned with mustard, thyme, marjoram and salt and pepper. Brown veal well in fat in a skillet. When browned and drained on absorbent paper, sprinkle each slice with lemon rind. Cook frozen peas according to instructions on the package.

In a large, shallow casserole, place layers of the veal, noodles, onions and peas. Melt butter in a saucepan, then blend in flour. Add milk and 2 cups of the reserved onion broth, stirring constantly until creamy smooth. Add salt and pepper to taste. Pour this mixture into the casserole. Bake in a preheated 375° oven until bubbly, about 45 minutes. Garnish with olives (or you can add them before baking).

Serves 8.

For a nice addition, serve a delicately herbed beet and egg salad with onion rings and melba toast. Some chilled fruit would make an excellent dessert.

VEAL SCALLOPS IN CASSEROLE

1½ pounds veal scallops
2 medium-size onions, sliced
3 or 4 tomatoes, peeled and
   sliced
4 to 6 carrots, scraped and
   very thinly sliced
½ to ¾ pound mushrooms,
   sliced

½ cup pitted ripe olives,
   sliced or whole
Salt and freshly ground
   black pepper to taste
Butter
½ cup red wine or stock
3 medium potatoes,
   thinly sliced

Arrange the veal and the vegetables in alternate layers in a buttered casserole, seasoning each layer with salt and pepper. Dot generously with butter and pour on wine. Cover and bake in a preheated 300° oven for 1 hour. Add layer of potatoes. Sprinkle with salt and pepper and brush well with butter. Increase the oven heat to 350° and cook uncovered 35 to 45 minutes or until the potatoes are cooked through and crusted.

Serves 4.

You'll need nothing with this dish but a salad—perhaps endive and celery—and crisp French bread. For dessert try lemon sherbet.

VEAL SCALOPPINE MARSALA

2 pounds thin veal scallops
Flour
Salt and freshly ground
   black pepper
Paprika
¼ cup butter
3 or 4 shallots, finely chopped

1 cup sliced mushrooms
¼ cup Marsala
1 tablespoon chopped parsley
A few fresh tarragon leaves
   or small pinch dried
   tarragon
¼ cup Marsala

Dredge veal with flour seasoned with salt, pepper and paprika. In a large skillet, sauté veal slowly in butter. When nicely browned, remove to a serving dish and keep warm.

Add the shallots to the butter remaining in the skillet and sauté for 2 minutes. Add mushrooms and stir well. Add the Marsala and allow it to cook down for a few minutes. Add the parsley, tarragon and remaining Marsala. Allow all to boil up for 1 to 2 minutes before pouring over the scallops.

Serves 4.

A risotto goes well with scaloppine, as does a spinach salad. A bowl of fresh fruit and an Italian cheese like Bel Paese or Fontina make a pleasant end to the meal.

ROAST LAMB BOUQUETIERE

6-pound leg of lamb	2 tablespoons butter
2 cloves garlic, quartered	1 cup fine dry bread crumbs
1 teaspoon salt	¼ cup chopped parsley

Place leg of lamb on a rack in a roasting pan, fat side up. With skewer or sharp knife, make small, deep cuts in the lamb and push a piece of garlic into each cut. Rub lamb with salt. If you have a meat thermometer, insert it so the bulb is in center of thickest portion of the meat (make sure it does not touch fat or bone). Roast in a 325° oven about 2½ hours or until thermometer has reached the temperature at which lamb is done—140° for rare, 160° for medium.

Melt butter and combine with bread crumbs. Remove lamb from oven. Preheat broiler. Coat lamb with buttered crumbs; broil 6 inches from source of heat for about 4 minutes or until crumbs are golden brown. Place on a hot platter; sprinkle with chopped parsley.

Serves 8.

Surround the lamb with new potatoes and glazed carrots. You might serve fresh peas and buttered spinach as well. Have strawberries for dessert—perhaps strawberries romanoff.

CASSOULET CASTELNAUDARY

1 quart dried white beans	3-pound lamb shoulder roast
1¼ pounds pork skin, cut into small pieces	1½-pound pork shoulder or loin roast
2 teaspoons salt	5- to 6-pound duckling
1 teaspoon freshly ground black pepper	1 pound garlic sausage or salami, thinly sliced
2 cloves garlic, chopped	Buttered bread crumbs

The Gascon section of France is known for its wonderful variety of cassoulets. The famous one from Castelnaudary is one of the greatest of these, a tasty dish for hearty eaters. (It's even better when it's cooked ahead of time and then warmed up, so you can carry it to a picnic and reheat it.)

Wash beans well. Cover them with water and let them soak overnight. Drain and cover with fresh water. Add pork skin, salt, pepper and garlic. Bring to a boil, reduce heat to low and continue simmering until beans are soft.

While the beans are cooking, salt and pepper lamb, pork and duckling. Roast them together in a preheated 300° oven until just barely cooked through, about 1½ hours. Cut the meats in slices or small pieces.

Drain the beans, reserving their cooking liquid. Line a large casserole with beans. Add a layer of pork, then a layer of beans, then a layer of lamb, a layer of beans, a layer of duck, a layer of beans, a layer of garlic sausage and finally a layer of beans. Top with buttered crumbs and add 2 cups of the reserved bean liquid to casserole. Let it stand for a few hours to mellow. Bake in a 350° oven for 2 to 3 hours, adding more bean liquid to the casserole if it seems to get too dry.

Serves 10 to 12.

All you need with this great cassoulet is a big green salad and some French bread. Try melon balls for dessert.

LAMB STEAKS INDIENNE

1 clove garlic, crushed
1 tablespoon curry powder
  Powdered ginger

¾ cup soy sauce
4 1-inch-thick lamb steaks

Combine garlic, curry powder, a bit of ginger and the soy sauce. Marinate the lamb steaks in this for 1 hour before broiling. Broil 3 inches from heat, turning once and basting frequently with marinade, until brown on outside and pink inside, about 10 minutes.

Serves 4.

Steamed rice goes well with these lamb steaks, and perhaps sautéed eggplant slices topped with grilled tomatoes. Baked rhubarb topped with fresh strawberries makes an agreeable dessert.

TARRAGON LAMB CHOPS

2 teaspoons dried tarragon
2 tablespoons white wine or
  vermouth

¼ cup butter
4 double loin lamb chops

Soak tarragon in wine or vermouth 30 minutes. Cream with butter. Make small incisions in the fat side of the lamb chops with a sharp knife and stuff bits of the tarragon butter in each chop. Broil and brush with remaining tarragon butter before serving.

Serves 4.

Buttered tiny carrots and a barley casserole would be good with the chops. Make a chocolate mousse for dessert.

LAMB WITH OKRA

1 pound okra	¼ cup olive oil
Vinegar	2 cloves garlic, finely chopped
1½ pounds lamb shoulder	1 large onion, thinly sliced
Flour	1½ cups tomato juice
Salt and freshly ground black pepper	Juice of 1 lemon

Cut the stems off the okra and soak for ½ hour in a quart of lightly salted water with a little vinegar added.

Meanwhile, cut the lamb into serving-size portions. Dredge with flour and season to taste with salt and pepper. Heat the olive oil in a skillet and brown the lamb. Transfer it to a casserole as it is browned.

Add the garlic and onion to the olive oil. Sauté for a few minutes, then add to the meat. Add the drained okra, tomato juice and lemon juice. Cover and bake in a preheated 350° oven for 1½ to 2 hours or until the meat is tender and well blended with the seasonings.

Serves 4.

Serve this with browned rice baked in the oven in another casserole. A green salad with a bit of rosemary in the dressing would be good, and try a blueberry pie for dessert.

LAMB MEDITERRANEAN

3 pounds boned lamb shoulder, cut into serving-size pieces	3 tomatoes, sliced
Flour	2 cloves garlic, finely minced
½ cup butter	1 teaspoon tarragon
Salt and freshly ground black pepper to taste	1½ cups rice
	3 to 4 cups boiling chicken or beef broth or water

Dust lamb with flour and brown quickly in butter. Add salt and pepper to taste. Arrange the meat in a casserole and surround with a border of the tomatoes. Add garlic and tarragon. Weight the meat down with a heavy plate or lid. Cover the casserole and bake in a preheated 325° oven for 1 hour. Remove cover and weight. Add rice and enough boiling broth to cover the meat and rice. Cover and continue baking until the rice is tender, 25 to 30 minutes.

Serves 6.

Serve with minted fresh peas and a celery salad. Have lemon meringue pie for dessert.

LAMB AND ARTICHOKE CASSEROLE

3 medium onions, chopped
4 tablespoons butter
2 pounds lamb shoulder or leg,
   cubed
   Flour
   Salt and freshly ground
      black pepper to taste

1 or 2 cloves garlic,
   finely minced
1 tablespoon chopped mint
   Water or beef bouillon
3 medium artichokes or
   1 package (12 ounces)
      frozen artichoke hearts
   Lemon juice

Brown onions lightly in butter. Lightly dust lamb with flour. Brown quickly in the skillet with the onions. Transfer the contents of the skillet to a casserole. Add salt and pepper to taste, garlic and mint. Add enough water to cover the meat. Cover tightly and bake in a preheated 350° oven for 40 minutes.

Carefully trim the artichokes, cut them into sixths and remove the choke sections. Sprinkle them with lemon juice so that they do not discolor. Add to the lamb casserole. Cover casserole with a piece of aluminum foil and place cover on top. Continue baking until the lamb is tender and the artichokes cooked, about 1 hour. Rectify seasoning and serve.

Serves 4.

This is excellent with either a rice pilaf or small new potatoes cooked in their jackets. For the salad, serve sliced tomatoes and paper-thin sweet onion slices with an olive oil and vinegar dressing; and this is a good spot for a dessert like lemon pudding.

BRAISED BREAST OF LAMB

3 pounds lamb breast,
  cut into bite-size pieces
  Flour
4 tablespoons butter
2 cloves garlic, finely cut
1 teaspoon salt

1 teaspoon freshly ground
  black pepper
1 cup tomato puree
½ cup dry vermouth
2 onions, thinly sliced
  Pinch thyme
4 carrots, cut into strips

Dredge lamb in flour, then sear in butter. Remove to a casserole with remaining ingredients. Cover and bake in a preheated 350° oven for 45 minutes to 1 hour or until the lamb is tender and the carrots cooked through.

Serves 6.

This is delicious with baked potatoes cooked in the oven at the same time, and watercress without dressing—this because the lamb dish is on the rich side.

MOUSSAKA

2 large eggplants
4 tablespoons olive oil
3 cloves garlic, finely chopped
  Salt and freshly ground
  black pepper to taste
2 cups chopped leftover lamb
  (or any other meat)
1 onion, finely chopped

1 large or 2 small tomatoes,
  peeled, seeded and chopped
1 teaspoon thyme
½ cup bread crumbs
2 eggs, slightly beaten
¼ cup dry white wine or
  vermouth
  Butter

There are about a million ways of preparing this delicious casserole dish. We shall give only the basic recipe and let you develop variations as you choose.

Peel eggplants, keeping skin in large pieces. Cut their meat into cubes and sauté in oil and garlic. Cover and simmer 15 minutes. Add salt and pepper to taste. Combine lamb with onion, tomatoes, thyme, bread crumbs and eggs.

Parboil pieces of eggplant skin for 10 minutes. Oil a casserole well with olive oil. Then line with a layer of the eggplant skin so that the pieces overlap each other with the skin side out. (Cover the sides as well as the bottom of the casserole.) Now add the eggplant-meat mixture together with wine; dot with butter. Cover and bake in a preheated 325° oven for 35 to 45 minutes. Remove from oven and invert casserole onto a heated platter so that the moussaka will turn out like a molded dish.

Serves 4 to 6.

Have a casserole of rice, baked with chicken broth and a few pine nuts. For a fine dessert, serve an apricot Bavarian cream.

LAMBURGERS

---

1 pound ground shoulder or leg of lamb	¼ cup chopped parsley Salt and freshly ground black pepper to taste
1 small onion, chopped	
1 clove garlic, grated	4 strips bacon
1 egg	Melted butter

Combine ground lamb with onion, garlic, egg, parsley, salt and pepper. Form into 4 patties. Wrap the edge of each patty with a strip of bacon and fasten with a wooden pick. Brush patties with melted butter. Grill, broil or panbroil as you would hamburgers; you will find that lamburgers are juicier if they are rare in the middle. Remove the wooden picks before serving.

Serves 4.

These are good with warmed Middle Eastern bread and tomatoes stuffed with rice. Have cut-up fresh fruit and some crisp little cookies for dessert.

PRUNE-STUFFED ROAST PORK

Choose about a 4-pound pork loin roast and have the chine bone loosened. Make a deep cut through the center of the meat. Insert about 15 dried prunes that have been pitted and soaked in sherry for 12 hours. Press the roast together again and tie it securely in several places. Stand roast on the chine bone and roast in a pan at 325°, allowing about 25 minutes per pound. After 1 hour add 8 medium-size peeled potatoes that have been boiled for 10 minutes in salted water, then drained. Let them brown and continue cooking in the pork fat. Turn them once or twice during the cooking time. Salt and pepper the roast and the potatoes.

When the roast is done, remove to a hot platter and remove strings. Surround with the potatoes and pour the pan juices over the roast. Serve with additional prunes that have been soaked in the sherry and serve horseradish too.

Serves 6.

You might add braised celery as a side dish. Crème brûlée or an egg custard makes a luscious dessert.

TANGY PORK STEAK

2-pound pork steak, about 1 inch thick	½ cup chili sauce
Soy sauce	1 teaspoon sugar
1 tablespoon bacon fat or other fat	¼ teaspoon freshly ground black pepper
1 medium onion, thinly sliced	1 tablespoon prepared horseradish
1 cup tomato sauce	Pinch mace

Brush pork well on both sides with soy sauce and brown quickly in bacon fat. Place in a shallow casserole just slightly larger than the piece of meat. Cover with the sliced onion. Combine remaining ingredients and 1 tablespoon soy sauce. Pour this over the onion. Cover and bake in a preheated 350° oven for 1¼ hours or until the meat is tender, basting several times with the pan juices.

Serves 4 to 6.

With this savory dish, corn bread is superb. Let thinly sliced apples sautéed in butter and a cucumber salad round out the meal. And for dessert, serve pears with cheese or try pear dumplings.

PORK STEAK WITH SAUERKRAUT AND APPLES

2- to 2½-pound pork steak	3 medium onions, sliced
Fat	Salt and freshly ground
1½ pounds (3 cups) sauerkraut	black pepper
6 medium apples, peeled,	Butter
cored and sliced	Sweet cider

Brown pork quickly in a little fat in a heavy skillet. Now arrange in layers in a large casserole half the sauerkraut, half the apples, the pork steak, the onions, the remaining sauerkraut and the remaining apples. Sprinkle each layer lightly with salt and heavily with pepper. Dot the layers occasionally with butter and dot the top lavishly. Pour on sweet cider to not quite cover. Cover and bake for 2 hours in a 325° oven.

Serves 4 to 6.

Fix stuffed baked potatoes: Combine the potato, sour cream, cheese, a little mustard, and salt and pepper to taste; reheat quickly in the oven. Serve a green salad, perhaps with a green-onion dressing. A coffee ice is a refreshing dessert.

ITALIAN-STYLE PORK CHOPS

4 pork chops, cut about
   2½ inches thick
½ teaspoon salt
½ cup chopped mushrooms
¼ cup tomato puree

3 cloves garlic, finely chopped
1 tablespoon chopped fresh
   basil leaves or
   1½ teaspoons dried basil
Garlic-flavored olive oil

Cut a pocket in each chop. Combine salt, mushrooms, tomato puree, garlic and basil; blend. Add a spoonful of this mixture to the pocket in each chop. Grill slowly for about 1 hour or broil until done, basting with a little olive oil from time to time.

Serves 4.

Serve with buttered noodles topped with Parmesan cheese. A good green salad dressed with oil and vinegar is refreshing. Melon makes a nice dessert if you can find a good ripe one in the market.

PORK CHOPS WITH SWEET POTATOES

3 cups mashed sweet potatoes
Butter
Pinch nutmeg or mace
2 large onions, thinly sliced
4 to 6 large pork chops

3 tart apples, peeled, cored
   and sliced
Salt and freshly ground
   black pepper

Flavor the sweet potatoes with plenty of butter and a pinch of nutmeg. Now arrange in layers in a buttered casserole half the onions, half the sweet potatoes, the pork chops, the apples, the remaining onions and the remaining sweet potatoes. Sprinkle each layer with salt and pepper and dot with butter. Dot the top layer with extra butter. Cover and bake for 2 hours in a 325° oven.

Serves 4 to 6.

Try a celery salad with mustard dressing and some good hot corn bread with this one. Fresh grapes are dessert.

JAMBALAYA

1 pound lean pork, cubed
1 large onion, chopped
1 tablespoon butter
1 tablespoon olive oil
1 pound ham, cubed
4 cups water
½ cup sherry
1 teaspoon dry mustard

½ teaspoon celery salt
½ teaspoon summer savory
½ teaspoon thyme
¼ teaspoon freshly ground
    black pepper
1½ cups long-grain rice,
    well washed

Brown pork in a skillet with onion, butter and olive oil. Just before it is browned, add ham and fry for 3 minutes. Place the meat and onion in a large casserole. To the grease in the skillet, add water, sherry, mustard, celery salt, savory, thyme and pepper. Cover the meat and onion with rice. Bring the contents of the skillet to a boil and pour over the rice. Stir once into the ham and pork. Cover the casserole and bake in a preheated 325° oven for 40 minutes. Stir once with a long-tined fork about halfway through the cooking.

Serves 6.

Grilled tomatoes and a green salad are good accompaniments. Finish the meal with an upside-down apple tart.

SAUSAGES IN WHITE WINE

1½ cups dry white wine
 1 cup beef bouillon
 1 cup diced carrots
16 small white onions

Salt and freshly ground
 black pepper to taste
 1 pound good-size link pork
 sausages

In a casserole, combine wine, bouillon, carrots and onions. Add salt and pepper to taste. Cover and cook in a preheated 350° oven for 30 minutes. Meanwhile, brown sausages in a skillet to render off part of their grease but not quite cook them through. Add them to casserole when it has cooked 30 minutes; then cook, uncovered, for another 30 minutes or until vegetables are tender and sausages cooked through.

Serves 4.

Serve this with fluffy mashed potatoes with plenty of butter. Celery and endive stalks in place of salad, whole wheat rolls and a lemon meringue pie will fill out the meal.

HAM LOAF

---

2 pounds ground smoked ham
1 pound ground fat pork
2 teaspoons dry mustard
¼ teaspoon ground cloves
½ cup mayonnaise
½ cup chopped parsley

½ teaspoon freshly ground
 black pepper
2 eggs, beaten
 Pork skin or salt pork strips
 Pineapple juice, sherry or
 dry vermouth

Combine ham with pork. Season with mustard, cloves, mayonnaise, parsley, pepper and eggs; mix well. Shape into a loaf, place in a baking pan and top with pork skin. Bake for 1½ to 2 hours in a 325° oven, basting occasionally with pineapple juice.

Serves 4 to 6.

Excellent with this would be sautéed pineapple slices and fried sweet potatoes. Serve cheese and crisp bread as a finish to the meal.

HAM AND CHEESE PIE

3 tablespoons butter
2 eggs, separated
¾ cup grated Parmesan cheese

1 cup diced cooked ham
1 teaspoon Dijon mustard

Cream butter until soft. Beat in egg yolks until fluffy. Add cheese, ham and mustard. Then beat egg whites until stiff and fold into ham-cheese mixture. Pour all into a well-greased shallow casserole and bake in a preheated 350° oven until puffy and lightly browned on top, 30 to 35 minutes.

Serves 2.

Crusty French bread, warmed in the oven and served with an herb butter, would go well here, as would a romaine salad. Try fresh pears for dessert.

LIVER ROLLS

1 pound calf's or
    lamb's liver, thinly sliced

¼ pound prosciutto or other
    ham, thinly sliced
    Butter

Cover each slice of liver with a slice of prosciutto. Roll the liver slices around the prosciutto and secure with small skewers or wooden picks. Sauté in butter over medium heat, turning several times. The liver should be pinky rare and the ham just heated through.

Serves 4.

With this serve boiled new potatoes with butter and some sautéed sliced onions. Lemon sherbet would be a good dessert.

TRIPE A LA NICOISE

¼ cup olive oil
4 medium onions, sliced
1 pound tomatoes, peeled
   and seeded
½ teaspoon thyme
½ teaspoon rosemary
   Salt and freshly ground
   black pepper to taste

4 cups rosé wine
1 calf's or pig's foot,
   split in half
2 pounds tripe, cut into
   1x3-inch strips
   Grated Parmesan cheese

Heat olive oil in a deep casserole (preferably flameproof earthenware) and sauté onions lightly. Add tomatoes, thyme, rosemary, salt and pepper. Simmer until well blended. Add wine; stir until smooth. Then add calf's foot and tripe and mix well. Cover and bake in a 325° oven for 4 to 5 hours. Correct the seasoning and sprinkle liberally with Parmesan cheese.

Serves 4 to 6.

Boiled or fluffy baked potatoes always seem necessary with tripe, as does French bread. Somehow it also always needs the crispness of a green salad. For dessert serve an apple pudding.

SAVORY BEEF HEART

1 beef heart (about 4 pounds)
2 cups fresh bread crumbs
1 medium onion, finely chopped
3 tablespoons bacon fat
½ teaspoon powdered ginger
   Salt and freshly ground
   black pepper to taste
   Flour

¼ cup bacon fat
2 cups veal or beef stock
   (1 cup dry red wine
   may be substituted for
   1 cup stock)
12 small white onions
8 carrots, quartered
   Butter

Wash and trim heart carefully. Slit open and wash again. Combine the fresh bread crumbs, onion, bacon fat, ginger and salt and pepper to taste to make a dressing. Stuff the heart with this.

Reshape heart and tie firmly with string. Dredge in flour and brown quickly in a skillet in the bacon fat. Place in a casserole and pour in the stock. Cover and bake in a preheated 350° oven for 2½ to 3 hours, frequently turning the heart and basting with the pan juices. Add the onions and carrots to the casserole for the last 45 minutes. When done, thicken the juices slightly with small balls of equal quantities of flour and butter that have been mashed together.

Serves 4.

Tiny young turnips and mushrooms, served together with plenty of parsley and butter, are elegant with this too-often-forgotten dish. Pickles seem to be in order. And for dessert, try meringue shells filled with chocolate ice cream and topped with whipped cream.

RABBIT NICOISE

1 rabbit, cut into serving portions	1 jigger Cognac
Butter	Salt and freshly ground black pepper
½ clove garlic, crushed	6 sweet Italian sausages
2 tablespoons olive oil	½ pound mushrooms, sliced
2 cups dry red wine	

Brown rabbit well on all sides in butter. Place in a casserole with garlic, olive oil, wine and Cognac. Sprinkle with salt and pepper. Cover and bake in a 325° oven for 1½ hours. Brown sausages in butter. Add to casserole with mushrooms. Cook 30 minutes more and serve.

Serves 4 to 6.

Glazed white onions are good with this unusual dish. And to round out an unusual meal, you might try polenta. Red wine would go well too; and dessert could be fresh or thawed frozen peaches flavored with a dash of bourbon.

VENISON RAGOUT

2 cups red wine
¼ cup red wine vinegar
2 cloves garlic, minced
2 medium onions, chopped
½ cup olive oil
2 or 3 sprigs celery leaves
3 juniper berries, ground
½ teaspoon freshly ground
   black pepper
   Juice and grated rind of
   1 medium-size lemon
1 small bay leaf
¼ teaspoon thyme

⅛ teaspoon oregano
3 pounds venison, cut into
   1- to 1½-inch pieces
½ cup fine strips salt pork
2 cups stewed tomatoes, or 3
   tablespoons tomato puree
   mixed with ½ to 1 cup meat
   stock
   Red wine and meat stock,
   mixed half and half
   (if needed)
1 tablespoon butter
2 tablespoons flour

Combine the first 12 ingredients. Soak the venison in this marinade for 24 to 48 hours in a cool place, turning occasionally to coat each piece well. (Always remember that the marinade is a flavoring as well as a tenderizing device.)

At cooking time, render fat from salt pork strips. Brown venison in the pork fat, then remove all together to a casserole with a tight cover. Add the marinade to browned meat, along with tomatoes. Simmer 1 to 1½ hours or until tender. (If meat becomes too dry, add wine-stock mixture as required.) Mash together butter and flour to make a paste, then add to casserole, stirring until thickened. Taste for seasoning.

Serves 6 to 8.

Serve this with wild rice with mushrooms and some buttered turnips. A hot mince pie gives you the perfect dessert.

5
POULTRY

STUFFED CHICKEN IN WHITE WINE

1 medium onion, finely chopped
1 tablespoon butter
3½ cups stale or toasted bread crumbs
1 cup finely cut celery
1 teaspoon thyme
1 teaspoon marjoram
1 tablespoon chopped parsley
¼ cup butter
Salt and freshly ground black pepper to taste
4-pound roasting chicken
¼ cup olive oil
1 cup dry white wine
12 small white onions
15 small new potatoes, peeled
12 mushrooms
Parsley sprig

Make this basic bread stuffing: Sauté onion in butter until transparent. Blend with bread crumbs, celery, thyme, marjoram and parsley. Cut in butter. Add salt and pepper to taste. Stuff chicken and truss.

Brown chicken well in olive oil in skillet; reserve oil. Place chicken in a casserole with ½ cup wine. Cover and cook in a preheated 325° oven for 45 minutes.

In the meantime, sauté onions and potatoes in skillet in oil remaining from browning chicken. Add salt and pepper to taste. The vegetables should be nicely browned and partially cooked. Remove casserole from oven and add potatoes, onions, mushrooms, parsley, salt and pepper. Add remaining wine, cover and replace in oven. Cook until chicken is tender and vegetables are cooked through, about 30 minutes.

Serves 4 to 6.

This is delicious with crisp slices of cornmeal mush, sautéed in butter. Have tiny French peas with small white onions. A chocolate mousse would wind things up nicely.

CHICKEN NEWCASTLE

4 ounces noodles
1 quart chicken broth
  Salt and freshly ground
    black pepper to taste
¼ pound chicken livers, chopped
¼ pound mushrooms, sliced
2 tablespoons butter or other
    fat

½ teaspoon nutmeg
½ cup grated Parmesan cheese
½ cup heavy cream
  4-pound roasting chicken
6 tablespoons butter or other
    fat

Prepare a stuffing as follows: Cook noodles in chicken broth until tender (about 9 minutes). Add salt and pepper to taste. Drain and reserve the broth. Sauté chicken livers and mushrooms in butter in a skillet over low heat for 3 minutes. Add to the noodles with nutmeg, cheese and cream. Blend well and stuff the chicken. Sew up the vent and truss the chicken.

Brown the chicken quickly in the butter, turning the chicken on all sides to achieve an evenness of color. Place in a casserole with 1 cup of the reserved chicken broth. Cover and bake in a preheated 350° oven for 1½ hours. Baste occasionally with a little broth—every 20 minutes should be sufficient.

Serves 4 to 6.

Try a rutabaga puree with this, and fried tomatoes, either green or ripe. Pineapple with thawed frozen raspberries makes a refreshing dessert.

CHICKEN TYROL

4-pound roasting chicken
1 veal knuckle, cracked
1 teaspoon thyme
1 bay leaf
1 leek
Salt and freshly ground
black pepper
½ pound lean pork, ground
¼ pound veal, ground
¼ pound smoked ham, ground
1 cup buttered bread crumbs
4 chicken livers, minced
3 shallots, minced
Thyme
Pork casing or cotton cloth
4 carrots, quartered
8 small white onions
8 mushroom caps

Make an incision down the backbone of the chicken with a small sharp knife. Remove backbone, ribs and breastbone, leaving the wing and leg bones in place. Reserve the removed bones. You will reshape the chicken after stuffing it.

Now make a bouillon of the chicken bones, veal knuckle, a bouquet garni of thyme, bay leaf and leek, and salt and pepper. Add enough water to cover the bones well and simmer 1½ hours.

For the stuffing, blend together pork, veal, ham, crumbs, livers and shallots. Season with salt, pepper and a bit of thyme. Stuff the chicken. Then mold the bird into shape, sew the back and vent closed and wrap and tie the bird securely in the pork casing.

Strain the bouillon into a casserole. Place the chicken in this and let it poach, uncovered, for 1 to 1½ hours in a preheated 300° oven. Add the carrots, onions and mushroom caps to the bouillon for the last 30 minutes of cooking. At the same time, unwrap the chicken and return it to the casserole to finish poaching.

Serves 4.

A spinach salad dressed with a mustardy vinaigrette goes well with this. Have a plum tart for dessert.

CHICKEN CASSEROLE WITH PINEAPPLE

5 tablespoons butter or
   other fat
2 2-pound broiler-fryer
   chickens, quartered
   Salt to taste
½ cup pineapple juice

1 cup cubed pineapple
2 thin slices lemon
½ cup pineapple juice
1 cup blanched toasted
   almonds
½ cup pineapple juice

Melt the butter in a skillet and brown the chicken well on all sides, adding salt to taste. Place the chicken in a casserole with pineapple juice. Cover and bake in a preheated 350° oven for 25 minutes.

Add the cubed pineapple, lemon slices and pineapple juice and bake for 15 minutes. Test for tenderness. Add the almonds and pineapple juice. Uncover and bake for 5 minutes.

Serves 4.

Baked sweet potatoes are fine with this. And serve grilled ripe tomatoes with fresh basil and a touch of olive oil. Instead of dessert, have some toasted French bread with cheese—some Brie or Schloss and perhaps some Liederkranz.

SAUTEED CHICKEN WITH BACON

2 2-pound broiler-fryer chickens,
    cut into quarters
    or serving pieces
  Flour
  Salt and freshly ground
    black pepper

8 slices bacon
4 shallots or green onions,
    finely chopped
2 tablespoons chopped parsley
1 tablespoon flour
1 cup heavy cream

Dredge chicken in flour seasoned with salt and pepper. Cook bacon in a large skillet until crisp. Remove bacon to absorbent paper; cool and crumble. Brown chicken pieces on both sides in hot bacon fat. Reduce heat and continue cooking gently for about 12 minutes. Then add shallots and parsley; mix well with chicken pieces. Cover and continue cooking until chicken is tender, about 10 minutes.

Remove chicken to a hot platter. Add the flour to the juices in the skillet, blend in, then add the cream and mix well. Pour this over the chicken and sprinkle the crumbled bacon over the top.

Serves 4.

Serve with mashed potatoes and buttered fresh peas. A blackberry tart is a tasty dessert.

CHICKEN SAUTE WITH CABBAGE

2 broiler-fryer chickens (about
    2½ pounds each), quartered
6 tablespoons butter
1 medium head cabbage, thinly
    shredded

  Salt to taste
  Marjoram
1 cup heavy cream

Brown chicken quarters well in 4 tablespoons butter. Reduce heat, cover and cook for 25 to 30 minutes. Meanwhile, cook cabbage in boiling water until just limp; drain. Add salt, 2 tablespoons butter and a little marjoram. When the chicken is just about tender, add seasoned cabbage and cream. Cover and simmer for 5 minutes.

Serves 4 to 6.

Serve with plain boiled potatoes and a cucumber salad. For dessert, have chocolate pots de crème.

CHICKEN WITH OLIVES

---

2 broiler-fryer chickens (about 2½ pounds each), quartered
Flour
Salt and freshly ground black pepper
½ cup butter
½ cup olive oil

2 teaspoons thyme or oregano
1 cup dry white wine
2 cups sliced mushrooms
2 or more cups green olives (the small Spanish ones are best)

Dredge chicken lightly in flour. Salt and pepper it well. Combine butter and olive oil in a skillet; heat until butter melts. Brown chicken pieces quickly in fat until they are a rich, golden brown. Add thyme and wine. Cover, reduce the heat and cook for about 20 minutes. Remove cover and turn chicken pieces. Add mushrooms and olives to pan. Let them blend well with juices in pan; cook for about 10 minutes. Remove chicken to a hot platter and pour mushroom and olive sauce over it.

Serves 8.

Serve with rice and zucchini sautéed with oil and garlic. A Grand Marnier soufflé makes a festive dessert.

CHICKEN CASSEROLE WITH RICE

4-pound roasting chicken,
  cut into serving pieces
Lemon juice
Seasoned flour
¼ pound bacon, slivered
6 carrots, scraped and quartered
3 medium onions, sliced

1 large clove garlic, chopped
1 teaspoon tarragon
1½ cups rice
2 or more cups chicken broth
  (made from giblets and
  neck of chicken)
½ cup chopped parsley

Rub chicken pieces with lemon juice, then dredge in seasoned flour. Fry bacon in a skillet until crisp. Remove to a large casserole. Brown chicken in bacon fat, a few pieces at a time, so that it achieves an even color. Place in casserole with carrots, onions, garlic and tarragon.

Brown rice in skillet in which chicken was browned, adding more fat if necessary. Add rice to casserole with enough broth to cover completely. Add parsley. Cover and bake in a preheated 375° oven for 1 hour or until the rice is thoroughly cooked and the liquid entirely cooked away. (If broth cooks away before rice is soft, add a little more.)

Serves 4.

This is a complete one-dish meal. Serve it with a bowl of radishes, green onions and celery. Hot rolls and sweet butter are always good. Fresh pineapple makes a pleasant ending to the meal.

CHICKEN MEXICAN

5-pound roasting chicken or capon, cut into serving pieces
Seasoned flour
Olive oil
3 medium onions, finely chopped
3 cloves garlic, finely chopped
¾ cup dry red wine, heated
1 teaspoon sesame seeds
½ teaspoon caraway seeds
Pinch mace
Pinch marjoram
2 cups boiling chicken broth
Salt and freshly ground black pepper to taste
1 cup blanched almonds
1 cup pitted green olives
4 tablespoons sweet chili powder
Cornmeal

Dredge chicken in seasoned flour. Oil a large earthenware casserole well and arrange chicken in it. Cook, uncovered, in a preheated 500° oven for 20 minutes. Lower the heat to 325° and add onions, garlic, wine, sesame seeds, caraway seeds, mace, marjoram and boiling broth. Season with salt and pepper to taste. Cover and bake 20 minutes. Then add almonds, olives and chili powder. Re-cover and bake 20 minutes longer, basting the chicken occasionally.

To thicken the sauce to desired consistency, add cornmeal mixed with cold water. In doing so, be sure to stir constantly until thickening takes place, for the meal has a tendency to go to the bottom of the pot or casserole and stick there. Bake 20 minutes or until chicken is tender. Put aside and reheat when needed, for this dish is much better made ahead of time.

Serves 4 to 6.

For this you might have some tortillas, frijoles refritos (refried beans) and sautéed green peppers. For dessert, why not serve a delicious baked caramel custard?

COUNTRY CHICKEN

4- to 5-pound roasting chicken,
  cut into serving pieces
Seasoned flour
6 tablespoons butter
12 small white onions
12 small carrots
3 tablespoons chopped parsley
  Sprig or pinch of thyme

2 cups chicken broth, made
  from the chicken's giblets
4 tablespoons flour
2 cups milk
  Salt and freshly ground
    black pepper to taste
  Nutmeg

Dredge chicken pieces in seasoned flour. Melt butter in a skillet and brown the chicken pieces, a few at a time, on all sides. Place the browned chicken in a flameproof casserole, reserving the fat in the skillet. Place the onions, carrots, parsley and thyme in the casserole. Pour in the chicken broth. Cover and bake in a preheated 350° oven for 45 minutes.

While the chicken is cooking, prepare the sauce. Add the flour to the fat in the skillet and blend well; you will need at least 4 tablespoons of fat, so add more if necessary. Add milk slowly, stirring constantly, and cook over low heat until mixture thickens. Add salt and pepper and a sprinkle of nutmeg. When chicken is done, remove with the vegetables to a hot platter, pour the sauce over and serve.

Serves 4 to 6.

Mashed potatoes and green beans are good accompaniments. The perfect dessert is an apple pie.

CHICKEN WITH LENTILS

2 cups lentils
2 quarts water
1½ teaspoons salt
2 cloves garlic, finely chopped
1 bay leaf
    4-pound roasting chicken,
      cut into serving pieces

Seasoned flour
6 tablespoons butter
    Salt and freshly ground
      black pepper
    Chicken broth or bouillon
      (if needed)
5 slices bacon

Soak lentils in water overnight or for 5 to 6 hours (unless quick-cooking ones are used). Place soaked lentils in a deep kettle with their soaking water. If there's not enough water to cover by about 1 inch, add boiling water. Add salt, garlic and bay leaf. Simmer gently until lentils are tender, about 1 hour, testing after 45 minutes.

Dredge chicken in seasoned flour. Brown quickly in butter. Salt and pepper heavily, place chicken pieces in a casserole and cover with lentils and liquid. If there is not enough liquid, add chicken broth. Cover and bake in a 350° oven for 1 to 1½ hours or until chicken is tender. Add additional liquid if the casserole cooks dry. Uncover and top with bacon for the last 15 minutes of cooking.

Serves 4 to 6.

Small young heads of Boston lettuce, braised in butter, are excellent with this. And sour gherkins are an added touch. For an elegant but easy dessert, poach some peaches in a sugar syrup.

CHICKEN WITH NOODLES AND ALMONDS

4- to 5-pound chicken
1 carrot, sliced
1 onion, sliced
6 peppercorns
½ bay leaf
½ cup dry white wine
  (optional)
1 pound noodles

¾ cup blanched almonds
  Olive oil
4 tablespoons flour
4 tablespoons butter
1 cup heavy cream
1 tablespoon grated shallot
  Salt and freshly ground
    black pepper to taste

Simmer chicken until tender in lightly salted water to cover with carrot, onion, peppercorns and bay leaf. Skin and remove meat from bones. Set meat aside and return skin and bones to broth to cook 20 minutes longer. Here, if you wish, add wine. Strain the broth and set aside.

Boil noodles until just tender, 10 to 12 minutes. Drain, rinse with cold water and drain again. Brown blanched almonds lightly in a little oil. Now make a rich cream sauce using flour, butter, 1 cup of the strained chicken stock and heavy cream. Add shallot. Season to taste with salt and pepper.

Arrange noodles, chicken and almonds in lightly packed layers in a buttered casserole. Pour on sauce and bake in a preheated 350° oven for 20 minutes. Just before serving, add several tablespoons of the reserved chicken stock to moisten.

Serves 4 to 6.

This casserole is on the rich side, so accompany it with something simple: buttered green beans and crisp, hot toast. Baked custard could be your dessert, and coffee is always in order.

CHICKEN WITH WALNUTS

2½-pound chicken	½ cup shredded ham
1 pound shelled walnuts	Soy sauce
Peanut oil	Dry sherry
6 tablespoons peanut oil	Fresh coriander (also called
4 green onions, finely shredded	Chinese parsley or
½ cup shredded snow peas	*cilantro*) if available

Cut chicken from bones and then cut into cubes 1 inch or smaller. Blanch walnuts in boiling water and rub skins off. Deep fry in hot peanut oil at 350° for 2 to 3 minutes. Drain on absorbent paper. Heat 6 tablespoons peanut oil in a skillet. Add onions, snow peas, ham and chicken pieces. Sauté until chicken is just lightly browned and cooked through, about 8 minutes. Add soy sauce to taste, a little sherry and the walnuts. Decorate with a little fresh coriander.

Serves 4.

Serve with fluffy rice and buttered broccoli. Have sliced pears with cream for dessert.

CHICKEN HASH MORNAY

2½ cups diced cooked chicken	2½ cups hot Mornay Sauce (page 157)
1 cup chopped mushrooms, sautéed in 2 tablespoons butter	Buttered bread crumbs Grated Swiss or Parmesan cheese or a mixture of both

---

Combine chicken and sautéed mushrooms. Blend in hot sauce and pour mixture into a well-greased casserole. Sprinkle with buttered crumbs and grated cheese and slip under the broiler until heated through and browned.

Serves 4.

This will be good with a puree of spinach and some fried tomatoes. Have some crisply toasted bread, and brandied figs for dessert.

SALMI OF CHICKEN

---

2 shallots, finely chopped
2 tablespoons butter
½ cup dry vermouth
½ cup pitted ripe olives,
  sliced or whole
  Pinch thyme
  Pinch rosemary
2 cups diced cooked chicken

1 cup leftover or
  canned chicken gravy
  Salt and freshly ground
  black pepper to taste
1 teaspoon lemon juice
1 package (12 ounces)
  frozen peas, thawed

Sauté shallots in butter until just transparent. Add vermouth, olives, thyme and rosemary. Blend in chicken and gravy. Season with salt, pepper and lemon juice. Pour into a casserole and mix in peas. Bake for 35 to 40 minutes in a preheated 350° oven.

Serves 4.

Buttered noodles and a green salad go well with this dish. For dessert, try sliced oranges sprinkled with confectioners' sugar and cinnamon.

ROAST TURKEY SESAME

---

3 pounds turkey parts
  Flour
1 egg, beaten with a
  little water
1 cup sesame seeds

½ cup butter
¼ cup Cognac, warmed
¾ cup dry white wine
½ cup butter, melted
¾ cup heavy cream

For this dish select those portions of the bird you like best—breast, wings, second joints or legs. Dredge the turkey well in flour, then dip in egg. Roll the pieces in sesame seeds until they are thoroughly and thickly coated. Brown them quickly in butter on all sides, but do not let the butter burn. Then transfer them to a large casserole, pour Cognac over them and blaze.

Roast uncovered in a 325° oven for 1½ hours, basting occasionally with a mixture of wine and butter. Add cream to the pan. Blend with the pan juices and baste the turkey well. Return to the oven and cook for 20 minutes more.

Serves 4 to 6.

Crisp fried potatoes with plenty of parsley are very good indeed with this turkey. And have a salad of cucumber, onions and tomato. Baked bananas with rum make a nice dessert.

TURKEY-OLIVE CASSEROLE

5- to 6-pound fryer-roaster turkey, cut into serving pieces
Seasoned flour
½ cup butter
½ pound bacon, cut into tiny slivers

½ cup chopped shallots or green onions
2 cups canned Italian-style tomatoes
1 cup sliced ripe olives

Dredge turkey pieces in seasoned flour. In a large skillet, melt butter and brown turkey a few pieces at a time. Place in a large casserole. Add bacon, shallots, tomatoes and olives. Cover casserole and cook in a 325° oven until turkey is tender, 1½ to 2 hours. Taste for seasoning.

Serves 8.

Serve with hot corn bread. Start dinner with a platter of raw vegetables and leave them on the table. Dessert should be light, like fresh pineapple with kirsch and small cookies.

TURKEY-SWEET POTATO PIE

---

3 cups diced cooked turkey
3 cups well-crumbled leftover
   turkey stuffing
2 eggs
1 cup milk
½ teaspoon salt

¼ teaspoon freshly ground
   black pepper
2 cups cooked sweet potatoes
¼ cup butter
Pinch mace or nutmeg

In a well-buttered casserole, combine turkey with stuffing. Beat eggs with milk, salt and pepper. Pour over the turkey mixture. Mash sweet potatoes and whip them until light and fluffy with butter. Add mace and season with salt and pepper to taste. Spread over turkey and dot with additional butter. Bake in a preheated 375° oven for 35 to 40 minutes.

Serves 4 to 6.

Start this dinner with a good clear soup. Serve braised Brussels sprouts and celery with the main course. Mincemeat turnovers for dessert could give your meal a party touch, and cheese would add an extra fillip.

TURKEY-RICE CASSEROLE

---

2 medium onions, chopped
4 tablespoons butter
½ pound mushrooms, sliced
2 cups diced cooked turkey
½ cup diced ham
1 cup crumbled leftover
   turkey stuffing
2 tablespoons chopped parsley

Pinch thyme
Salt and freshly ground
   black pepper
1 cup rice
1 tablespoon curry powder
2 cups turkey or chicken broth,
   heated

In a skillet, sauté onions in 3 tablespoons butter until just tender. Add mushrooms and sauté for 2 minutes. Combine in a deep casserole with turkey, ham, stuffing, parsley, thyme and salt and pepper.

In the skillet in which onions were sautéed, brown rice with 1 table-spoon butter and curry powder. Add browned rice to casserole and pour in broth. Cover and place in a preheated 375° oven and cook until rice is tender and broth is absorbed, about 40 minutes. (If broth is absorbed before rice is cooked, add more, but heat before adding to casserole.)

Serves 4 to 6.

Serve with chutney and a cucumber salad. Try a seasonal fruit like persimmons for dessert.

DUCK IN RED WINE

5- to 6-pound duckling, cut into serving pieces	2 sprigs parsley
½ clove garlic, minced	1 small bay leaf
2 tablespoons flour	½ teaspoon thyme
2 cups dry red wine	1 teaspoon salt
8 mushrooms, sliced	8 small white onions
	8 small carrots, scraped

Remove skin and fat from duck. Cook skin and fat with giblets and neck, simmering for about 1 hour. Skim off fat and reserve it; reserve giblets.

In a large frying pan, brown the duck pieces over low heat in 2 table-spoons of duck fat. Place the browned pieces in a casserole. To the fat in the frying pan add garlic and cook for 1 minute. Stir in flour. Add wine, mushrooms, parsley, bay leaf, thyme and salt. Bring this to a boil, stirring constantly until sauce thickens.

Place white onions, carrots and duck giblets in casserole with the duck. Top with sauce. Cover tightly. Bake in a 350° oven until duck and vegetables are done, about 1¼ hours.

Serves 4.

Barley, rice or wild rice would be a pleasant addition to this fine duck—and tiny new turnips in a generous gift of butter. An apple crisp or apple tart—hot and spicy—might be your dessert.

DUCK CASSEROLE
WITH CARAWAY AND RED CABBAGE

5- to 6-pound duckling,
  cut into serving pieces
Seasoned flour
6 tablespoons fat
1 onion, finely chopped
Caraway seeds
Good pinch basil

½ cup water
1 medium head red cabbage
3 tablespoons wine vinegar
2 tablespoons brown sugar
  Salt and freshly ground
    black pepper to taste

Dredge duck parts well in seasoned flour. Brown in a skillet in 4 table-spoons fat. Transfer to a deep casserole. Add onion, a sprinkling of caraway seeds and basil. Pour on water. Cover and place in a pre-heated 350° oven for 30 minutes.

While duck is cooking, shred cabbage, discarding hard center core. Add 2 tablespoons fat to skillet in which duck was browned and add shredded cabbage. Let it cook down for 10 minutes, tossing frequently with a fork. Add vinegar, brown sugar and salt and pepper to taste. Simmer 5 minutes more.

Combine cabbage with duck in casserole. Cover and cook until duck is tender, about 1 hour after cabbage has been added.

Serves 4.

Good fluffy rice would be fine with this casserole, with chopped green onions and raw mushrooms vinaigrette on the side. Crisp French rolls are always an addition. And for dessert, melon.

DUCK WITH PINTO BEANS

2 cups dried brown pinto beans
¼ pound salt pork, diced small
   5- to 6-pound duckling,
     cut into serving pieces
   Seasoned flour

1 medium onion, thinly sliced
   Basil
   Freshly ground black pepper
   Dry mustard

Soak the beans overnight in cold water to cover. Drain, cover with lightly salted water and simmer until just tender. Drain, reserving the liquid. Place half the beans in a casserole; reserve the remaining beans.

Fry the salt pork in a skillet until crisp. Place the bits of pork in the casserole with the beans. Dredge the duck in the seasoned flour and brown quickly in the pork fat. Transfer to the casserole.

Add the onion, a pinch of basil, a sprinkling of pepper and a generous couple of pinches of dry mustard. Cover with the reserved beans and season again with basil, pepper and mustard. Bring the reserved bean liquid to a boil and pour into the casserole just to cover the beans. Cover and bake in a preheated 350° oven until the duck and beans are well done, 1½ to 2 hours. Add more bean liquid if necessary, but the casserole should not have too much liquid when done.

Serves 4 to 6.

This would be excellent with some buttered turnips and an endive and beet salad. And what better way to wind it up than with an apple charlotte?

DUCK SALAD WITH ORANGE

Roast 2 ducklings in a 325° oven for 2 to 2½ hours or until done, basting every few minutes with thawed frozen orange juice concentrate. Season with salt. Cool. Cut into quarters with carving shears or sharp kitchen scissors, then cut each quarter into 2 pieces. Arrange the pieces on a bed of greens and surround with alternating slices of orange and onion, both sliced paper thin. In the center, put a large bowl of mayonnaise with a great deal of chopped parsley and a little grated orange rind mixed into it.

Serves 4.

Crisp French bread is all you need to serve with the main course. For dessert, have coffee ice cream.

ROAST GOOSE
WITH POTATO AND NUT STUFFING

3 cups lightly whipped potatoes	1 teaspoon salt
2 cups dry bread crumbs	1 teaspoon freshly ground
1 teaspoon rosemary	black pepper
1 cup finely diced onion	3 tablespoons butter, melted
1 cup coarsely chopped walnuts	8- to 10-pound goose
or pecans	Dry white wine

Combine potatoes with crumbs, rosemary, onion, walnuts, salt, pepper and butter. Blend well and stuff goose with this mixture. Close vent of goose. Place it on a rack in a roasting pan and bake in a preheated 450° oven for 30 minutes. Reduce heat to 325° and roast for another 2 to 2½ hours or until the breast is tender and the skin crisp. Basting the skin with white wine will give it a good color. Pour off the goose fat as it accumulates in pan and save it for cooking. Salt and pepper the goose just before removing from oven.

Serves 6.

Serve with mashed yellow turnips and sautéed apple slices. Make dessert mixed fruits with kirsch.

PIGEON CASSEROLE

4 wood pigeons or squabs
4 small onions
  Parsley sprigs
6 strips bacon, diced
1 clove garlic, minced
1 medium onion, finely chopped

1 sprig thyme
  Pinch basil
1 cup sliced mushrooms
2 cups canned solid-pack
  tomatoes
1 tablespoon brown sugar

Stuff each pigeon with a small onion and several sprigs of parsley. Fry the bacon in a skillet until the fat is rendered out, then sauté the garlic briefly over low heat. Remove bacon and garlic from the skillet and brown the pigeons in the fat very quickly on all sides.

Place the birds, bacon and garlic in a deep casserole with the onion, thyme, basil, mushrooms, tomatoes and brown sugar. Cover and bake in a preheated 350° oven for about 1 hour or until birds are tender. Taste for seasoning before serving.

Serves 4.

Buttered noodles are a must with this. Try some mashed yellow turnips for your vegetable. Crêpes suzette would make a festive dessert.

PHEASANT WITH SAUERKRAUT

2 pounds sauerkraut,
  drained
2 cups chicken broth
1 cup white wine
  Few juniper berries

½ teaspoon caraway seeds
2 pheasants
¼ cup butter or other fat
  Salt and freshly ground
  black pepper to taste

Place sauerkraut in a deep casserole (preferably flameproof earthenware). Add broth, wine, juniper berries and caraway seeds. Cover and simmer for 1 hour.

Clean pheasants. Brown well on all sides in butter. Add salt and pepper to taste. When the birds are thoroughly browned, place them in the casserole with the sauerkraut. Cover and place in a preheated 350° oven. Bake until pheasants are tender, about 35 to 45 minutes. Serve pheasants on a hot platter, surrounded with sauerkraut.

Serves 4.

Boiled potatoes and a green salad should be included in this menu. Baked quinces and heavy cream would make an agreeable dessert.

6
EGGS AND CHEESE

BASIC SOUFFLE

3 tablespoons butter
3 tablespoons flour
¾ cup milk
   Salt and freshly ground
     black pepper to taste

1 cup cooked chopped turkey or
   chicken, flaked fish, flaked or
   chopped shellfish—any
   leftover meat or fish
4 eggs, separated

Melt butter in the upper part of a double boiler and blend in flour. Gradually add milk, stirring constantly. Add salt and pepper to taste and remove from fire. Blend in chopped meat or fish. Other things may be added to give zest to the soufflé. For example, try adding a few chopped olives with duck or chicken. Pieces of mushroom or roasted Italian peppers are good in many meat or fish soufflés.

Beat egg yolks until thick and lemon-colored. Add to mixture in double boiler and blend thoroughly. Beat egg whites until stiff and fold into mixture. (Additional egg whites, if you want to be luxurious, will make the soufflé lighter.) Fold half of the whites in first, rather thoroughly. Then add the rest, folding very gently. Be sure you fold; don't stir.

Pour into a greased 1- to 1½-quart soufflé dish or casserole. Bake in a preheated 375° oven for 25 to 35 minutes, depending on the state of doneness you like: Some people prefer the French soufflé, which is slightly runny in the center; some prefer it well done all the way through. Either way, serve the soufflé the instant it comes from the oven.

Serves 4.

Serve the soufflé plain or with your favorite sauce: tomato, cheese, mushroom or whatever you think would make a good combination of flavors. A tossed green salad or coleslaw goes well with any soufflé. Fruit desserts—as simple or elaborate as you wish—are a good ending.

CHEESE SOUFFLE

3 tablespoons butter
2 tablespoons flour
1 cup milk, scalded
1 teaspoon salt

Few grains cayenne pepper
½ cup grated sharp Cheddar
   cheese
4 eggs, separated

Melt butter in upper part of double boiler. Add flour and stir with wooden spoon until well blended and smooth. Gradually add milk, stirring constantly. Continue to stir until mixture thickens and becomes smooth. Add salt, cayenne and cheese. Continue stirring until cheese is melted. Remove from fire.

Beat egg yolks until light and lemon-colored. Pour the slightly cooled cheese mixture onto egg yolks, stirring constantly. Cool for a short time.

Now beat egg whites until very stiff, then fold into mixture. Pour into buttered 1-quart soufflé dish or casserole. Bake in a preheated 375° oven until well browned, 35 to 40 minutes. Serve at once.

Serves 4.

Crisp bacon goes well with a cheese soufflé, and fried tomatoes, or a tomato salad. Fresh or stewed fruit makes a pleasing dessert.

COTTAGE CHEESE PUDDING

1 pound (2 cups) cottage cheese
2 tablespoons chopped chives
1 egg, beaten
2 tablespoons heavy cream

Salt and freshly ground
   black pepper to taste
Cayenne pepper or
   Tabasco sauce to taste

Combine all ingredients. Pour into a well-greased casserole and bake in a preheated 350° oven for 20 minutes.

Serves 4.

This pudding makes a nice light meal served with a salad of marinated mixed vegetables. Have applesauce and cookies for dessert.

CHEESE PUDDING

⅓ cup milk
1 cup fresh bread crumbs
1 cup grated Cheddar cheese
½ teaspoon dry mustard

Salt and freshly ground
   black pepper to taste
2 eggs, well beaten

In a small saucepan, heat the milk until just barely hot. Pour into a mixing bowl over the bread crumbs. Add the remaining ingredients and blend all together thoroughly. Pour into a buttered casserole. Bake in a preheated 350° oven for 30 minutes.

Serves 4.

Serve this with a salad of greens and cherry tomatoes. For dessert, try something rich: an angel cake, with some of the center torn into chunks, mixed with whipped cream and raspberries, then forced back into the cake again. Top with raspberry-flavored whipped cream.

EGGS FOO YONG

6 green onions,
   cut into fine 2-inch strips
3 tablespoons peanut oil
1 cup shredded ham
½ cup shredded bamboo shoots
1½ cups bean sprouts

8 water chestnuts, thinly sliced
2 tablespoons soy sauce
1 teaspoon monosodium
   glutamate
9 eggs

In a large skillet, sauté the green onions in oil. Add ham, bamboo shoots, bean sprouts, water chestnuts, soy sauce and monosodium glutamate. Toss well and taste for seasoning; it may need more soy.

Beat eggs until light and fluffy. Pour carefully over mixture in pan. Cook for 2 to 3 minutes on top of the stove, then run under broiler just until eggs are set and cooked through. Serve from skillet.

Serves 6.

Serve an endive and watercress salad with this dish. Finish with litchis—fresh if you can get them, canned if not.

7
VEGETABLES

GREEN BEAN CASSEROLE WITH TOMATOES

1 cup chopped onion	1 bay leaf
2 tablespoons bacon fat	1 tablespoon chopped parsley
2 cups canned tomatoes	1 clove garlic, crushed
1 cup diced celery	1½ pounds green beans, Frenched
½ green pepper, chopped	Grated sharp Cheddar cheese
1 tablespoon sugar	Buttered bread crumbs
1 teaspoon salt	
½ teaspoon freshly ground black pepper	

Sauté onion in bacon fat. When light brown, add tomatoes, celery and green pepper. Season with sugar, salt, pepper, bay leaf, parsley and garlic. Simmer for 30 minutes, stirring frequently. Remove bay leaf and garlic.

Boil green beans in lightly salted water until tender; drain. Place alternate layers of beans, tomato sauce and cheese in a buttered casserole. Top with buttered crumbs and bake in a preheated 325° oven for 25 minutes.

Serves 6.

GREEN BEANS WITH SOUR CREAM

1½ pounds green beans, cut up	Salt and freshly ground black pepper to taste
4 tablespoons olive oil	1 tablespoon grated onion
1½ cups dairy sour cream	Dry bread crumbs

Boil the beans in salted water until tender and drain. Pour the oil into a casserole. Add the beans, sour cream, salt and pepper to taste and onion. Combine this mixture well and sprinkle with crumbs. Bake in a preheated 300° oven for 30 minutes.

Serves 4 to 6.

GREEN BEANS DUPONT

2 quarts water
1½-inch cube salt pork
2 pounds green beans, cut up
2 tablespoons butter
2 tablespoons flour

1 cup milk
½ cup grated sharp cheese
Salt and freshly ground
  black pepper to taste
Paprika

Bring water to a boil in a large pot and cook salt pork 5 to 10 minutes. Add beans and cook until just barely tender, not limp, 15 to 30 minutes. Drain beans and salt pork, reserving ¼ cup of the cooking liquid. Place beans in a lightly greased casserole. Dice salt pork very fine and fry in a skillet until crisp; drain on absorbent paper and reserve.

Melt butter in top of a double boiler. Blend in flour and gradually stir in milk and reserved vegetable liquid. Cook, stirring, until thickened. Blend in cheese and season with salt and pepper to taste.

Pour the cheese mixture over the beans in the casserole. Sprinkle with more grated cheese, the salt pork dice and the paprika. Bake in a preheated 350° oven for 20 minutes.

Serves 8.

SUCCOTASH CASSEROLE

1 cup cooked lima beans
1 cup cooked whole-kernel corn
1 cup cooked Frenched
  green beans

1 cup (or more if desired)
  Mornay Sauce (page 157)
Buttered bread crumbs
Grated Parmesan cheese

Combine lima beans, corn and green beans in a casserole. Cover with Mornay sauce and sprinkle liberally with crumbs and cheese. Brown in a preheated 400° oven for 15 to 20 minutes before serving.

Serves 6.

KIDNEY BEAN CASSEROLE

1 clove garlic, crushed
3 tablespoons olive oil
1 pound dried kidney beans, soaked and simmered until nearly tender

½ cup dry red wine
2 tablespoons minced parsley
½ cup small pimiento-stuffed green olives, halved through their equators

In a flameproof casserole, cook the garlic in the oil until soft but not browned. Mix in the remaining ingredients. Cover and bake in a preheated 350° oven for about 45 minutes. If the beans need more liquid, add additional wine during the baking period.

Serves 6.

KIDNEY BEAN CASSEROLE WITH ONIONS

1 pound dried kidney beans
4 strips lean salt pork
1 bay leaf
1 large onion, grated
1 large onion, thinly sliced

Salt and freshly ground black pepper
½ cup minced parsley
½ cup dry red wine for each cup cooked beans

Cook kidney beans in lightly salted water with salt pork, bay leaf and grated onion. When beans are almost tender, drain and discard bay leaf. Reserve the salt pork.

Arrange beans in alternate layers in a casserole with sliced onion. Sprinkle each layer lightly with salt and pepper and generously with parsley. End with a layer of beans at top. Dice the salt pork and dot over casserole. Pour wine over all. Cover and bake in a preheated 350° oven until beans are tender, 30 to 40 minutes.

Serves 4 to 6.

PUREE OF SPLIT PEAS

1 cup dried split peas
2 cups water
1 stalk celery, diced
1 carrot, diced
½ teaspoon salt

¼ teaspoon freshly ground
   black pepper
3 strips bacon,
   cut into small bits
1 onion, chopped

Soak the split peas in the water overnight. Place the peas and the water in a saucepan and add the celery, carrot, salt and pepper. Simmer until it becomes a thick mush, then press through a sieve or force through a food mill.

Fry the bacon in a skillet until lightly browned. Remove the bacon bits and add to the peas. Sauté the onion in the bacon fat, then add the onion and fat to the peas. Pour into a greased casserole and bake in a preheated 350° oven for 15 to 20 minutes.

Serves 6.

CORN PUDDING

3 tablespoons butter
3 onions, sliced
1 green pepper, chopped
1 can (16 ounces)
   cream-style corn

½ teaspoon salt
¼ teaspoon freshly ground
   black pepper
   Pinch nutmeg
3 eggs, separated

Melt butter in a skillet and sauté onions and green pepper until tender. Add corn, salt, pepper and nutmeg. Heat thoroughly and remove from fire. Beat egg yolks well and stir in. Beat egg whites until stiff. Pour corn mixture into a greased casserole and fold in egg whites. Bake in a preheated 300° oven until pudding sets, 15 minutes; do not let it get too dry.

Serves 4.

CORN-STUFFED PEPPERS

---

4 large or 8 small green peppers
2 cups canned or cooked fresh
  whole-kernel corn
¼ cup melted butter

Salt and freshly ground
  black pepper to taste
Buttered bread crumbs

Cut a slice off the stem end of each pepper and remove the seeds and membranes. Rinse with cold water. Parboil for about 5 minutes in a large saucepan of lightly salted water. Drain.

Combine the corn, butter, salt and pepper. Fill the pepper shells and top with the crumbs. Stand the peppers upright in a buttered casserole large enough to hold them all. Bake in a preheated 375° oven for 20 minutes.

Serves 4.

SAUTEED GREEN PEPPERS

Cut 6 green peppers into fine strips. Sauté gently in 6 tablespoons olive oil until just tender. Add salt to taste and 1 tablespoon red wine vinegar.

Serves 4.

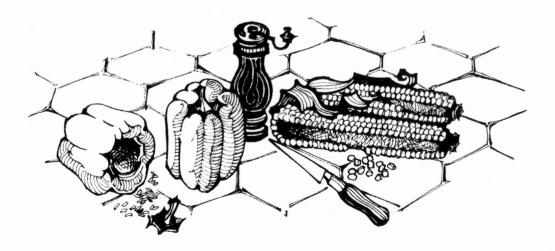

SPINACH CASSEROLE WITH MUSHROOMS

2 cups chopped cooked spinach
2 tablespoons butter, melted
1 teaspoon tarragon
½ teaspoon salt
   Few drops lemon juice

18 to 24 mushroom caps,
   sautéed in butter
4 eggs, well beaten
½ cup grated Parmesan cheese

Place spinach in a greased 2-quart casserole. Add butter, tarragon, salt and lemon juice. Place mushroom caps on top of spinach. Mix eggs with cheese and pour over mushrooms very gently. Bake in a preheated 350° oven until egg and cheese mixture is set, about 20 minutes.

Serves 4.

SPINACH SOUFFLE

3 tablespoons butter
3 tablespoons flour
1 cup milk
½ teaspoon salt

4 egg yolks
1 cup chopped cooked spinach
5 egg whites

Melt butter in the top of a double boiler. Blend in flour, stirring constantly. Add milk and continue stirring until mixture thickens. Season with salt. Cool slightly. Beat egg yolks, add to mixture and blend well. Fold in spinach. Beat egg whites until stiff and gently fold into spinach mixture. Pour into a well-buttered 2-quart soufflé dish or casserole. Bake in a preheated 375° oven until soufflé is lightly browned and well puffed, 35 to 50 minutes. Serve at once.

Serves 4.

BROCCOLI SOUFFLE

4 tablespoons butter
4 tablespoons flour
1 cup milk
4 eggs, separated

Salt and freshly ground
  black pepper to taste
1½ cups pureed cooked broccoli

Melt butter in the top of a double boiler. Blend in flour, stirring constantly. Add milk and continue stirring until mixture thickens. Remove from heat. Beat egg yolks and stir into mixture. Season to taste with salt and pepper and add broccoli puree. Mix thoroughly over gentle heat and remove from fire. Beat egg whites until stiff and fold into broccoli mixture. Pour into a buttered 2-quart soufflé dish. Bake in a preheated 375° oven for 35 minutes or until soufflé is lightly browned and well puffed. Serve immediately.

Serves 4.

BAKED CAULIFLOWER

Break 1 medium head cauliflower into flowerets and cook in lightly salted water until tender, about 15 minutes. Drain and arrange in a buttered casserole. Dot with butter and sprinkle liberally with grated Parmesan cheese. Add salt and freshly ground black pepper to taste. Top with buttered bread crumbs and additional cheese. Brown in a preheated 375° oven for about 10 minutes.

Serves 4.

Variations

Swiss Cauliflower: Cook and arrange flowerets as above. Pour over them 1 cup heavy cream and sprinkle with coarsely ground black pepper. Add grated Parmesan and Swiss cheese and top with buttered crumbs and more cheese. Bake in a preheated 450° oven until the flowerets are nicely browned and the cheese is melted, about 15 minutes.

CABBAGE CASSEROLE WITH SAUSAGE

Bacon slices
1 head cabbage, quartered
1 small onion, grated
½ teaspoon salt
½ teaspoon freshly ground
   black pepper

½ cup beef bouillon
1 pound medium-size
   country-style or Italian
   pork sausages

Line a good-size casserole with bacon slices. Place cabbage wedges on bacon. Add onion, salt, pepper and bouillon. Top with sausages. Cover and bake in a preheated 350° oven until cabbage is tender, about 1 hour.

Serves 4.

SAVOY CABBAGE AU GRATIN

1 medium head Savoy cabbage
2 cups chicken stock
4 tablespoons butter
4 tablespoons flour

1 cup milk
Buttered bread crumbs
Paper-thin lemon slices

Shred cabbage, discarding all of the center core. Bring chicken stock to a boil and cook cabbage until barely tender, about 6 minutes. Drain, reserving 1 cup of the stock.

In the top of a double boiler, melt butter and stir in flour. Gradually add the milk and the reserved stock. Cook, stirring, until thickened. Blend with cabbage and place in a well-greased casserole or baking dish. Top generously with buttered crumbs and a few lemon slices. Brown in a preheated 400° oven for about 20 minutes.

Serves 4.

RED CABBAGE IN WINE

1 medium head red cabbage
Salt and freshly ground
  black pepper
1½ cups dry red wine
1 tablespoon red wine vinegar
3 tablespoons soy sauce

1 tablespoon sugar
1 bay leaf, crushed
2 tablespoons butter,
  cut into bits
Grated fresh ginger
  (optional)

Wash cabbage thoroughly and remove outer leaves. Cut and shred as for coleslaw and place in a casserole. Sprinkle with salt and a generous amount of pepper. Then pour on wine, vinegar and soy sauce. Add sugar, bay leaf, butter and ginger. Toss all together and press down level in casserole. Cover and bake for 1½ to 2 hours in a 300° oven. Uncover and add a little more wine to moisten if necessary. Cook 20 minutes longer.

Serves 6.

SAUERKRAUT IN WHITE WINE

3 pounds sauerkraut
1 bottle (⅘ quart) dry
  white wine

3 cloves garlic, finely chopped
1 teaspoon freshly ground
  black pepper

Combine all ingredients in a large pot. Cover and simmer over a low flame for 4 to 6 hours, adding more wine if necessary.

Serves 6.

CELERY CASSEROLE WITH ALMONDS

2 heads celery
   Butter or olive oil
2 green peppers, cut into
   slivers
1 tablespoon chopped parsley
1 tablespoon chopped chives
½ clove garlic, finely minced

2 tablespoons olive oil
½ cup slivered blanched
   almonds, sautéed in
   butter
1 cup or more chicken or
   vegetable broth

Remove outer stalks and leaves from celery. Cut heads into quarters lengthwise and brown in butter. Place in a shallow casserole with green peppers, parsley, chives, garlic and olive oil. Top with almonds and pour on broth to a depth of ¼ inch in casserole. Cover and bake in a preheated 350° oven for 30 minutes, basting with liquid in casserole several times. Uncover, baste again and cook until celery is tender. Add more broth if needed during baking.

Serves 4.

BAKED ASPARAGUS WITH CHEESE

2 to 3 pounds asparagus
⅓ cup butter, melted,
   or olive oil

Grated Parmesan or
   Swiss cheese
Buttered bread crumbs

Cook asparagus and drain well. Grease a shallow oblong or oval casserole well with olive oil and place the asparagus in it. Sprinkle with butter, then add a generous topping of cheese. Cover with buttered crumbs and brown in a preheated 400° oven until the cheese melts, about 10 minutes.

Serves 4 to 6.

EGGPLANT BAKED IN CREAM

1 large eggplant,
    peeled and sliced
½ cup butter
    Salt and freshly ground
      black pepper

1 cup chopped walnuts or
    pecan halves
    Buttered bread crumbs,
      flavored lightly with mace
1 cup heavy cream (approxi-
    mately)

Brown eggplant slices quickly in butter. Place them in a shallow casserole, sprinkling each layer with salt, pepper and walnuts. Top generously with buttered crumbs. Pour on heavy cream to come just barely to level of eggplant. Bake in a preheated 325° oven for 20 to 25 minutes.

Serves 4 to 6.

ESCALLOPED EGGPLANT

1 large eggplant
½ small onion, chopped
1 green pepper, shredded
¼ cup butter

2 cups canned tomatoes
1 teaspoon salt
    Pinch nutmeg
    Buttered bread crumbs

Peel the eggplant and cut into 1-inch cubes. Let cubes soak 15 minutes in salted water, then drain and press them dry.

Sauté onion and green pepper in butter until onion is golden. Add tomatoes, salt and nutmeg. Let simmer until well blended, stirring from time to time. Add eggplant and simmer 30 minutes. Turn into a casserole, cover with buttered crumbs and bake in a preheated 350° oven until crumbs are brown, 25 to 30 minutes.

Serves 4.

EGGPLANT-TOMATO CASSEROLE

1 large eggplant,
   pared and sliced
  Olive oil
2 large onions, sliced
3 large tomatoes,
   peeled and sliced

2 medium green peppers,
   shredded
  Salt and freshly ground
   black pepper
  Butter
  Grated Parmesan cheese

In a skillet, brown the eggplant slices quickly in olive oil. Arrange in alternate layers in a well-greased casserole the eggplant, onions, tomatoes and green peppers. Season each layer with salt and pepper and dot with butter. Pour ¼ cup olive oil over all when the casserole is filled. Bake in a preheated 350° oven for 35 minutes or until tender. Sprinkle with grated Parmesan cheese and return casserole to the oven for 3 minutes.

Serves 4 to 6.

EGGPLANT AU GRATIN

1 large eggplant,
   peeled and sliced
  Flour
½ cup olive oil
2 large Spanish onions, sliced

  Salt and freshly ground
   black pepper to taste
¼ cup chopped parsley
  Buttered bread crumbs
  Butter

Dredge eggplant slices in flour and brown quickly in olive oil. Add onion slices and brown them. Arrange in a casserole, making alternate layers of eggplant and onion; season each layer to taste with salt and pepper. Sprinkle the top with parsley and cover with buttered crumbs. Dot with butter. Bake in a preheated 350° oven for 25 minutes or until vegetables are tender.

Serves 4 to 6.

MUSHROOMS IN WHITE WINE

1½ pounds mushrooms, sliced
½ cup butter
¼ cup chopped chives or
   green onions
¼ cup chopped parsley

Salt and freshly ground
   black pepper
½ cup dry white wine or
   vermouth
Chopped parsley

Sauté mushrooms quickly in butter. Add chives and parsley. Season with salt and pepper to taste, then add wine. Simmer for 5 minutes. Serve topped with additional parsley.

Serves 4 to 6.

SAVORY STUFFED TOMATOES

6 large beefsteak tomatoes
6 tablespoons butter, softened
1½ teaspoons anchovy paste
4 hard-cooked eggs,
   well chopped

2 teaspoons chopped chives
½ teaspoon dry mustard
   Dry bread crumbs

Cut off stem ends of tomatoes and carefully remove the pulp. Drain and chop the pulp; reserve. Blend butter and anchovy paste. Melt 4 tablespoons of the anchovy butter and brush the insides of tomatoes with it.

Combine eggs with chives, mustard and reserved tomato pulp. Blend well. Fill tomatoes lightly with mixture, sprinkle with bread crumbs and dot with remaining anchovy butter. Arrange tomatoes in a greased casserole and bake in a preheated 400° oven until browned, about 15 minutes.

Serves 6.

GREEK STUFFED TOMATOES

2 cloves garlic, finely cut
½ cup pine nuts
⅓ cup olive oil
1 cup long-grain rice,
　cooked until just tender
1 teaspoon salt

½ teaspoon freshly ground
　black pepper
½ teaspoon rosemary
6 large tomatoes
½ cup olive oil
¼ cup tomato puree
1 tablespoon lemon juice

Sauté garlic and pine nuts in olive oil. Combine with rice and season with salt, pepper and rosemary.

Cut the tops from tomatoes; scoop out seeds and pulp and discard. Stuff tomatoes with rice mixture. Place in a casserole. Combine olive oil, tomato puree and lemon juice and pour over tomatoes. Bake in a preheated 350° oven for 25 to 30 minutes, basting occasionally with pan juices. The tomatoes should be firm but cooked, and the rice should be well flavored by the other ingredients.

Serves 6.

Note: This same dish, with the addition of a little wine vinegar sprinkled over the cooked tomatoes, can be served cold as an hors d'oeuvre.

TOMATOES SICILIAN

6 ripe tomatoes
⅓ cup olive oil
3 or 4 whole allspice berries
1 teaspoon cinnamon
2 cloves garlic, chopped

¼ cup chopped parsley
½ cup chopped fresh basil
Salt and freshly ground
  black pepper to taste

Slice off top of each tomato. Heat olive oil in skillet. Add allspice, cinnamon, garlic, parsley, basil and salt and pepper to taste. Place tomatoes, cut side down, into the mixture. Cover the skillet and simmer very slowly for 30 to 35 minutes or until tomatoes are just hot through but not mushy. Serve with pan juices.

Serves 6.

TOMATO CASSEROLE WITH CELERY AND ONIONS

1 cup paper-thin slices celery
4 good-size tomatoes,
   thickly sliced
3 onions, cut into slivers
  Butter

Salt and freshly ground
  black pepper
Chopped fresh basil
Bread crumbs, browned in
  garlic butter

Arrange celery, tomatoes and onions in alternate layers in a buttered casserole, dotting each layer generously with butter and sprinkling with salt, pepper and a little basil. Top with a layer of bread crumbs. Bake in a preheated 350° oven until the vegetables are tender, 35 to 45 minutes.

Serves 4.

SCALLOPED TOMATOES

Buttered bread crumbs
1 can (1 pound 13 ounces)
   tomatoes
Salt and freshly ground
   black pepper to taste

Chopped fresh basil (dried
   can be substituted
   if necessary)
6 soda crackers,
   rolled into crumbs
Butter

Line a casserole with bread crumbs. Season tomatoes with salt, pepper and a touch of basil. Pour into casserole. Top with cracker crumbs and dot heavily with butter. Cover and bake in a preheated 350° oven for 35 minutes.

Serves 6 to 8.

BAKED ONIONS

4 medium Spanish onions
Salt and freshly ground
   black pepper
½ cup beef bouillon or
   consommé

Butter
1 cup grated sharp
   American cheese

Place onions in a buttered casserole that has a very tight cover. Season well with salt and pepper. Add bouillon and dot the tops of the onions with butter. Cover and bake in a preheated 350° oven until onions are just tender all the way through, about 1 hour. Remove cover and sprinkle with cheese. Return to oven uncovered or place under broiler until cheese melts.

Serves 4.

STUFFED ONIONS

4 large onions	½ pound well-seasoned sausage meat or link sausage

Parboil peeled onions for 20 minutes in salted boiling water. Drain and remove center portions with a sharp knife and a fork. Fill centers with sausage meat (remove the casing from the link sausage). Place in a buttered casserole. Bake in a preheated 375° oven until sausage is thoroughly cooked, 20 minutes.

Serves 4.

SCALLOPED ONIONS

Butter 4 large onions, sliced 2 cups cracker crumbs	Salt and freshly ground black pepper to taste 1 cup milk or light cream

Butter a casserole thoroughly. Place a layer of onions in it, then a sprinkling of cracker crumbs dotted with butter and seasoned with salt and pepper to taste, alternating onions and cracker crumbs until all are used. Add milk and dot with extra butter. Bake in a preheated 375° oven for 45 minutes.

Serves 4 to 6.

BABY ONIONS WITH MUSHROOMS AND SOUR CREAM

Combine boiled onions with sautéed fresh or canned button mushrooms. Season with salt and freshly ground black pepper. Toss with a little dairy sour cream.

SWEET AND SOUR ONIONS

4 very large onions, sliced	¼ cup butter
1 teaspoon salt	¼ cup sugar
¼ cup cider vinegar	¼ cup boiling water

Place onions in a casserole. Combine salt, vinegar, butter, sugar and boiling water. Pour this mixture over the onions in the casserole. Cover and bake in a preheated 300° oven for 1 hour.

Serves 4.

GREEN ONION QUICHE

3 bunches green onions, cut into 1-inch pieces (about 2 cups)	1½ cups light cream
	½ teaspoon salt
3 tablespoons butter	⅛ teaspoon freshly ground black pepper
Pastry for a one-crust pie	
3 eggs	3 strips bacon, diced

Gently sauté green onions in butter until tender. Let them cool. Line an 8-inch pie pan with the pastry. Cover the bottom of the pie shell with the green onions.

Beat eggs lightly with cream, salt and pepper. Pour egg mixture over green onions and sprinkle with bacon. Bake in a preheated 350° oven for 45 minutes or until custard is set and the top is a golden brown.

Serves 6.

CASSEROLE OF VEGETABLES
WITH CREAM AND CHEESE

---

1 head cauliflower
24 small white onions
1 can (12 ounces) tiny
   whole carrots, drained
   (reserve liquid)
1 can (12 ounces) tiny
   French peas, drained
   (reserve liquid)

2 tablespoons butter
2 tablespoons flour
1 cup light cream
½ cup grated Cheddar or
   Swiss cheese

Cook the cauliflower and parboil the onions in salted water. Drain. In the center of a casserole that can be used for a serving dish, place cauliflower. Surround this with carrots, peas and onions. In a saucepan, melt butter and stir in flour. Gradually add cream and 1 cup of the liquid from the carrots and peas. Stir until thickened. Add cheese; blend well until cheese melts. Pour this sauce over vegetables. Sprinkle top with additional grated cheese. Run under broiler for a few minutes or bake in a preheated 400° oven for 5 to 8 minutes.

Serves 6.

PIZZA VEGETABLE CASSEROLE

1½ cups milk
1 cup water
1 teaspoon salt
¾ cup cream of rice
1 tablespoon chopped parsley
  Pinch thyme
3 tablespoons fat
¼ cup chopped onion

1 clove garlic, minced
¼ cup chopped celery
¼ cup chopped green pepper
½ cup chopped or
  sliced mushrooms
1 can (10½ ounces) condensed
  tomato soup
1 cup grated Cheddar cheese

Combine milk, water and salt in the top of a double boiler and heat over hot water. Slowly sprinkle in cream of rice; cook, stirring constantly, until slightly thickened, about 1 minute. Cover and cook gently 10 minutes longer. Stir in parsley and thyme. Pour into a 9-inch round cake pan, spread out thin and chill until firm.

Meanwhile heat fat in a skillet. Add onion, garlic, celery, green pepper and mushrooms. Sauté gently for 5 minutes. Add tomato soup and cheese. Stir together until the cheese is melted.

Cut the chilled cream of rice mixture into 6 to 8 wedges. Arrange these on a greased 12-inch pizza pan or other flat baking dish. Pour the sauce over all and bake in a preheated 375° oven until lightly browned, about 20 to 25 minutes. Serve immediately with a tossed salad.

Serves 6.

VEGETABLE CASSEROLE WITH HAM

24 very small white onions
 1 can (12 ounces) French peas
 1 medium head Boston lettuce
 1 cup shredded Virginia ham

¼ cup butter
  Salt and freshly ground
    black pepper to taste

This makes a splendid dish for outdoor eating, for it can be cooking in your kitchen oven while the chicken or turkey is on the grill.

Parboil onions in lightly salted water until just tender. Drain and set aside, reserving the liquor. Drain peas and set aside, adding their liquid to onion stock. Wash lettuce well; drain and shred.

Place vegetables and ham together in a casserole. Add butter, salt and pepper to onion-pea liquid; reduce to about 1 cup. Pour into the casserole and toss vegetables lightly so that they are well basted. Cover and bake in a preheated 350° oven for 20 minutes. Uncover and toss again before serving.

Serves 4 to 6.

8
POTATOES, RICE AND PASTA

NEW POTATOES VERTS

2 pounds new potatoes
¼ cup butter, melted

¼ cup minced parsley or chives, or ¼ cup minced parsley and 2 slices crisp bacon, crumbled

Wash and clean potatoes. Peel or scrape a strip around each one about ⅜ inch wide. Place them in a casserole with melted butter. Cover tightly and bake in a preheated 375° oven for about 30 minutes, shaking the casserole from time to time to turn the potatoes and coat them with butter. Test for tenderness, and if necessary, re-cover and cook until done. Sprinkle with parsley, or chives, or parsley and bacon.

Serves 4.

PARISIAN POTATOES

These are small new potatoes that are scraped and literally steamed in butter. Melt enough butter to cover the bottom of a skillet and roll tiny potatoes in the butter. Cover tightly and steam for 20 to 35 minutes or until just tender. Remove the cover, shake the pan several times and continue cooking until potatoes are delicately browned. Season to taste with salt and freshly ground black pepper.

Note: You can also parboil the scraped potatoes for 10 minutes, then drain and shake well in the pan to dry them. Transfer to a buttered skillet and sauté in butter until nicely browned and tender.

BRAISED POTATOES WITH SOUR CREAM

Peel and cook 6 to 8 medium potatoes in just enough broth to cover. Pour off most of the broth. Let potatoes dry for a minute in the pan over the flame. Season to taste with salt and freshly ground black pepper. Remove to a hot dish, cover with dairy sour cream and sprinkle with chopped parsley.

Serves 6.

GERMAN-FRIED POTATOES

Peel and slice potatoes about ⅛ inch thick. Estimate 1 medium potato per person. Heat ¼ cup butter, goose fat, bacon fat or lard for 4 potatoes. Cook potatoes over fairly brisk heat, turning often, until brown and just cooked through. Season to taste with salt and freshly ground black pepper.

POTATOES ANNA

4 large or 6 medium potatoes	Salt and freshly ground
Butter	black pepper

Peel potatoes and slice thin. Butter a shallow baking dish or casserole with sloping sides very thoroughly and place an even layer of potatoes on the bottom. Sprinkle with salt and pepper and dot with butter. Add another layer of potatoes and repeat the process.

Now stand a layer vertically around the sides. Then add layers in the middle with salt, pepper and butter as above until potatoes are used up. Dot the top with extra butter. Bake in a preheated 400° oven until potatoes are thoroughly cooked and crusted a golden brown, 40 to 50 minutes. These may be served from the casserole or baking dish, or the dish may be inverted and the potatoes turned out on a platter.

Serves 4.

POMMES BOULANGERE

Peel and slice 3 or 4 good-size potatoes. Melt 4 to 5 tablespoons butter, goose fat or beef fat in a heavy skillet. Arrange potatoes in a spiral over bottom of pan, starting from the center and building around the edges so that slices overlap. Arrange in layers. Cover with bouillon and dot with butter. Cook until bouillon is cooked away and potatoes are delicately browned at the edges. Season to taste with salt and freshly ground black pepper.

Serves 4.

SCALLOPED POTATOES

Peel and thinly slice 1 medium-large potato for each person to be served. Butter a casserole or baking dish well; arrange a layer of potatoes on the bottom, sprinkle with salt and freshly ground black pepper and dot with butter. Repeat this until all the potatoes are used. Then pour on milk to just below the level of the potatoes and dot the top with an extra quantity of butter. Cover and bake in a preheated 375° oven for about 30 minutes. Remove the cover and continue cooking until the potatoes are tender.

Variations

Scalloped Potatoes with Herbs: Sprinkle each layer with chopped parsley and chives, mixed, and with salt. Proceed as above.

Scalloped Potatoes Parmesan: Sprinkle each layer with grated Parmesan cheese and dot with butter. Top with cheese and extra butter and proceed as above.

Scalloped Potatoes with Onion: Alternate potato layers with thinly sliced onion and seasonings. Proceed as above.

Scalloped Potatoes with Ham: Alternate potato layers with cubed ham. Sprinkle each ham layer with chopped parsley, salt and freshly ground black pepper and add 1 teaspoon dry mustard to the milk before it is poured in. Bake as above.

Curried Scalloped Potatoes: Alternate layers of potatoes and thinly sliced onions. Add 2 teaspoons curry powder to the milk before pouring it in. Bake as above.

SAVOY POTATOES

Butter
6 potatoes
1 cup or more grated Gruyère
   or Swiss cheese

½ cup grated Parmesan cheese
Salt and freshly ground
   black pepper

These originated in the cheese country, which accounts for their luscious quality. Prepare them in the oven, in an electric skillet or in a heavy skillet over low flame. Butter the skillet or baking dish well. Peel and slice potatoes. Arrange a layer of potatoes, a layer of mixed cheeses, then sprinkle with salt and pepper and dot with butter. Continue this until potatoes are all used. Dot with butter and cover. Cook on low heat or in a preheated 325° oven until potatoes are tender. Remove cover and cook until they are nicely colored and the cheese has melted thoroughly.

Serves 6.

DELMONICO POTATOES

2 cups Béchamel Sauce
   (page 156)
Salt and freshly ground
   black pepper
Celery salt

2 cups diced boiled potatoes
1 cup grated Parmesan cheese
Paprika
Buttered bread crumbs

Season béchamel sauce with salt, pepper and celery salt. Arrange half the potatoes in a buttered casserole. Pour on 1 cup sauce and sprinkle with ½ cup cheese. Add the rest of the potatoes, the rest of the sauce and remaining cheese. Sprinkle with paprika and dust generously with buttered crumbs. Bake in a preheated 400° oven until sauce bubbles and crumbs are browned, 15 to 20 minutes.

Serves 4.

HASHED-IN-CREAM POTATOES

Peel cooked potatoes and chop rather coarsely. Sauté in fat until lightly browned. Sprinkle lightly—very lightly—with flour and pour in enough heavy cream to cover the potatoes. Season with salt and freshly ground black pepper. Simmer until the cream has cooked down and a crustiness has formed on the bottom of the pan.

CHEESED POTATOES

4 good-size potatoes, peeled	3 tablespoons butter
½ teaspoon salt	¼ cup heavy cream
¼ teaspoon freshly ground black pepper	1 cup grated sharp cheese

Boil potatoes in salted water until tender. Put them through a ricer into a mixing bowl with salt, pepper and butter. Whip all together and add heavy cream bit by bit until the potatoes are smooth. Fold in cheese and pile in a shallow casserole. Sprinkle the top lightly with additional grated cheese and brown in a preheated 400° oven before serving.

Serves 4 to 6.

WHIPPED POTATOES EN CASSEROLE

3 cups whipped potatoes	½ teaspoon salt
½ cup heavy cream	½ cup grated Parmesan cheese
¼ teaspoon freshly ground black pepper	

Pile the potatoes into a greased casserole. Whip the cream with the pepper and salt until stiff. Fold in the grated Parmesan. Spread over the potatoes. Bake in a preheated 350° oven until heated through and browned, about 10 minutes.

Serves 4 to 6.

POTATO PUFFS

---

5 or 6 medium potatoes,
   boiled and peeled
Butter

Salt and freshly ground
   black pepper
1 recipe Choux Paste
   (page 181)

Mash potatoes, adding butter. Salt and pepper well. For each cup of mashed potatoes, add a scant ½ cup of choux paste. Drop mixture by spoonfuls into deep hot fat at 360° and fry until brown and puffy. Serve with meats or as a snack with drinks.

Makes about 30 puffs.

Variation

Cheesed Potato Puffs: Add ½ cup grated Cheddar or Swiss cheese to the choux paste. Combine with potatoes and fry as above.

SWEET POTATOES TIPSY

---

2 cups hot riced sweet potatoes
3 tablespoons butter
½ teaspoon salt
¼ cup light cream

Freshly ground black pepper
¼ cup rum or sherry
   (approximately)

Place sweet potatoes in a mixing bowl with butter, salt, cream and a few grains pepper. Beat all together until light and fluffy, then beat in rum bit by bit until potatoes are creamy but still fluffy. Pile in a shallow casserole and brown in a hot oven before serving.

Serves 4.

SWEET WHIP

6 sweet potatoes
¾ cup port wine
6 tablespoons butter, melted

1 egg, beaten
Salt to taste

Boil sweet potatoes until very tender. Peel and mash them. Whip with port, butter, egg and salt to taste. Pile in a casserole and brush with additional melted butter. Bake in a preheated 450° oven for 8 minutes.

Serves 6 to 8.

RISOTTO

The risotto is the Italian version of a pilaf. It is a main course with the addition of one or two other dishes, or it may be an accompaniment for certain meat dishes.

Carolina rice is the best for this dish. Wash 1 cup of it thoroughly, then drain. Brown 1 medium-size onion lightly in ¼ cup butter. Add rice and cook gently with the onion for 4 minutes, tossing with a fork. Add 2 cups boiling bouillon and season to taste with salt and freshly ground black pepper. Turn into a casserole or baking dish. Bake uncovered in a preheated 350° oven for 17 to 20 minutes. Toss very gently with a fork from time to time. When dry and tender, add melted butter and grated Parmesan cheese to taste.

Serves 4.

Variations

Risotto Milanese: Prepare as above, but when adding bouillon, add pinch saffron, ½ cup sliced mushrooms and ¼ cup peeled, seeded and chopped tomato.

Greek Risotto: Add small bits garlic sausage or chorizo, green peas and chopped pimiento or green pepper after rice has been cooked.

Green Rice: Add 1 cup chopped parsley, 1 cup hot buttered freshly cooked tiny peas, ¼ cup butter, melted, and 1 tablespoon chopped chives to cooked rice. Toss lightly.

RICE PILAF

---

1 cup rice (Patna rice is best)
1 small onion, finely chopped
¼ cup butter
2 cups boiling bouillon

Salt and freshly ground
  black pepper to taste
Pinch thyme or oregano
Melted butter

Wash the rice thoroughly, then dry on a towel. Brown onion lightly in butter, adding rice just when onion begins to brown. Toss rice with a fork until it is just colored. Place in a baking dish or casserole. Add boiling bouillon, salt and pepper to taste and thyme. Cover and place in a preheated 350° oven. Bake until the liquid is entirely absorbed and the rice just tender, 20 to 25 minutes. Add melted butter before serving.

Serves 4.

Variations

Saffron Pilaf: Add a mere pinch of saffron to the rice just when you turn it into the baking dish.

Moghul Pilaf: Add toasted almonds, puffed raisins and peanuts, sautéed in oil and coarsely chopped, to the Saffron Pilaf. Serve with curry.

RICE PILAF IN CLAM JUICE

---

1 cup long-grain rice,
  well washed
3 tablespoons butter
1 tablespoon chopped parsley
1 tablespoon chopped chives

Dash Tabasco sauce
3 cups clam juice or a mixture
  of half clam juice and half
  chicken broth

Place rice in a flameproof casserole with butter, parsley, chives and Tabasco sauce. Add clam juice; cover and bring to a boil quickly on top of the stove. Place in a preheated 300° oven and bake until all the liquid has evaporated, about 40 minutes.

Serves 4.

BASIC BARLEY CASSEROLE

½ cup finely chopped onion
6 tablespoons butter
½ cup barley

Salt and freshly ground
    black pepper to taste
3 cups chicken broth or
    consommé

Sauté onion in butter until just barely soft. Add barley and brown lightly with onion. Season to taste with salt and pepper and pour into a casserole or baking dish. Add 1½ cups broth. Cover and bake in a preheated 350° oven 30 minutes. Add another 1½ cups broth and cook until liquid is completely absorbed.

Serves 6.

Variations

Barley with Mushrooms: Before adding the liquid, add ½ pound mushrooms, sliced, that have been lightly sautéed in ¼ cup butter.

Barley with Chicken Livers: Before adding the liquid, add ½ pound chicken livers that have been quickly sautéed in butter.

Barley with Almonds: Proceed as in basic recipe, adding sautéed mushrooms as in the Barley with Mushrooms variation. After adding liquid the second time, sprinkle top of casserole with ½ cup finely chopped toasted almonds.

Barley with Pine Nuts and Herbs: Before adding the liquid, add ½ cup finely chopped parsley, ¼ cup finely chopped chives or green onion and ½ cup pine nuts.

Barley for a Turkey Dinner: Just before serving, top barley with the following mixture: Sauté ½ pound mushrooms, finely chopped, in 6 tablespoons butter, simmering them down until almost black. Combine with ¼ cup chopped parsley and ½ cup slivered toasted almonds. This is delicious with any game or poultry dish.

Helen Brown's Chicken Gizzard Casserole: Cook until tender 1 pound chicken gizzards in 2 quarts water with 1 onion, studded with whole cloves, 1 teaspoon salt, a pinch thyme, 1 sprig parsley and a little celery. This will take 1 to 2 hours over moderate heat, depending on the gizzards. Add more water if necessary; you should have 3 cups left when finished cooking. When tender, drain gizzards, reserving broth. Slice and sauté them with onions. Then proceed as in basic recipe, using the reserved broth in place of the chicken broth.

NOODLES WITH CHEESE AND SOUR CREAM

½ pound thin noodles
1 cup cottage cheese
1 cup dairy sour cream
¼ teaspoon freshly ground
   black pepper
½ teaspoon salt

¼ cup butter, melted
½ teaspoon dry mustard
1 tablespoon Worcestershire
   sauce
Buttered bread crumbs

Boil noodles in lightly salted water until just tender. Rinse in cold water, then drain. Combine cottage cheese with sour cream, pepper, salt, butter, mustard and Worcestershire sauce. Add to cooked noodles and pour into a well-greased casserole. Top with buttered crumbs and bake in a 350° oven for 30 minutes.

Serves 4.

NOODLES FLORENTINE

½ pound noodles
¼ cup olive oil
1 clove garlic, finely chopped
½ cup grated mozzarella or
   Swiss cheese
   Freshly ground black pepper
1 package (12-ounce size)
   frozen spinach

1 teaspoon tarragon
1 tablespoon lemon juice
¼ cup butter
   Salt to taste
   Buttered toasted bread
   crumbs
   Grated Parmesan cheese

Cook noodles in boiling salted water until just tender; drain. Mix in olive oil, garlic, cheese and a good amount of pepper. Cook spinach according to directions on package. Drain and chop. Add tarragon, lemon juice, butter and salt to taste.

Make bed of spinach on bottom of a baking dish. Place noodles on top and sprinkle liberally with toasted crumbs and cheese. Run under broiler to heat noodles through and brown crumbs and cheese.

Serves 4.

NOODLE CASSEROLE WITH GREEN ONIONS

½ pound noodles
¼ cup butter
2 tablespoons olive oil
8 green onions (with about 1
    inch of the green tops),
    chopped

1 tablespoon chopped fresh
    tarragon
Salt and freshly ground
    black pepper to taste
Grated Parmesan cheese

Cook noodles in rapidly boiling salted water until just tender, 10 to 12 minutes. Drain, rinse with cold water and drain again. Place in a well-greased casserole and set aside.

Melt butter in a skillet with olive oil. Add green onions and tarragon. Sauté for 3 minutes. Pour over the noodles. Toss all together until well mixed and season with salt and pepper. Top with cheese and brown in a preheated 400° oven before serving.

Serves 4.

NOODLES AND POTATOES AL PESTO

¼ cup pine nuts
1 cup fresh basil leaves
1 cup parsley sprigs
3 cloves garlic
1 teaspoon salt

1 teaspoon black peppercorns
½ cup olive oil
6 medium potatoes, peeled and
    thinly sliced
½ pound noodles

To make pesto, blend in a blender or grind in a mortar pine nuts, basil, parsley, garlic, salt, peppercorns and olive oil.

Cook potatoes in boiling salted water until just pierceable. At the same time cook noodles in boiling salted water until just tender. Drain both and mix them together with the pesto.

Serves 6.

MACARONI CASSEROLE WITH BASIL

½ pound macaroni
2 tablespoons chopped parsley
1 tablespoon chopped fresh basil
⅓ cup grated Parmesan cheese

2 tablespoons olive oil
Salt and freshly ground
  black pepper
Grated Parmesan cheese

Cook macaroni in rapidly boiling salted water until just tender, about 10 minutes. Drain, rinse and drain again. Place in a greased casserole with parsley and basil. Sprinkle with cheese and olive oil. Season to taste with salt and pepper. Toss all together and top with more grated cheese. Cover and bake in a preheated 375° oven for 10 minutes.

Serves 4 to 6.

MACARONI CASSEROLE WITH SWISS CHEESE

Cook ½ pound macaroni in rapidly boiling salted water until just tender, about 10 minutes. Drain, rinse and drain again. Arrange in alternate layers in a greased casserole with grated Parmesan and imported Swiss cheese and sprinklings of salt and freshly ground black pepper. Top with an extra layer of cheese and buttered bread crumbs. Bake in a preheated 375° oven until the cheese is melted and the crumbs are brown, 20 to 25 minutes.

Serves 4.

SPAGHETTI WITH ANCHOVIES AND GARLIC

1½ pounds spaghetti
2 cloves garlic, finely chopped
⅔ cup olive oil
18 to 20 anchovy fillets, coarsely chopped

1 tablespoon chopped parsley
Pinch rosemary
Grated Parmesan or Romano cheese

Cook spaghetti in boiling salted water until just barely tender. While pasta cooks, prepare the sauce: Sauté garlic in olive oil and add anchovy fillets, parsley and rosemary; keep warm.

Drain the pasta and pour into a large serving bowl or arrange on a deep platter. Pour the sauce over it and toss to blend. Sprinkle heavily with cheese.

Serves 8.

9
SALADS AND SALAD DRESSINGS

BACON AND EGG SALAD

2 large heads romaine or
  leaf lettuce or 1 head lettuce
  and 1 bunch watercress
6 hard-cooked eggs, chopped
8 slices (½ pound) bacon,
  crisply fried and crumbled

Few green onions, chopped
Salt and freshly ground
  black pepper to taste
2 tablespoons vinegar
½ cup hot bacon fat

Break up lettuce in a large salad bowl. Sprinkle eggs and bacon on top of the lettuce. Add green onions. Season with salt (about 1 teaspoon) and pepper. Pour on vinegar and bacon fat. Mix tenderly but well.

Serves 6 to 8.

TOMATOES AND ONIONS VINAIGRETTE

4 large beefsteak tomatoes,
  peeled and thickly sliced
4 good-size sweet onions,
  thinly sliced

Salt and freshly ground
  black pepper
Basic French Dressing
  (page 152)

Arrange alternate slices of tomatoes and onions on a serving dish dressed with greens. Sprinkle a little salt and pepper over them. Serve with a bowl of French dressing.

Serves 6.

COLESLAW

1 medium head cabbage
½ cup Mayonnaise (page 153)
¾ cup dairy sour cream
1 teaspoon salt

1 tablespoon chopped fresh dill
  or 1 teaspoon dill seed,
  crushed
Freshly ground black pepper
  to taste

Shred cabbage very fine with a sharp knife. Prepare a dressing with the mayonnaise, sour cream, salt and dill. Add pepper to taste. Pour the dressing over the cabbage, toss well and let stand for 2 hours (to wilt the cabbage) before serving.

Serves 6.

Note: This is also good made with red cabbage or cauliflower instead of with cabbage.

VEGETABLE SALAD

Basic French Dressing
  (page 152)
Chopped chives or
  green onions
1 can (8 ounces) tiny whole
  green beans

1 can (8 ounces) tiny peas
  (petits pois)
1 can (8 ounces) tiny whole
  carrots or 1 can (8 ounces)
  tiny whole beets
Greens
Mayonnaise (page 153)

Season dressing with some chives. Drain the canned vegetables. Soak them in the dressing, turning now and then to be sure they get well bathed. Arrange the vegetables on a bed of greens and pass mayonnaise for those who want additional dressing.

Serves 6.

Note: You may prefer to cook your own vegetables the day before.

SHREDDED VEGETABLE SALAD
WITH LEMON DRESSING

6 carrots
6 beets
2 green peppers
2 cucumbers
½ small head red cabbage
1 cup cottage cheese
1 cup dairy sour cream

Lemon juice to taste
Salt and freshly ground
   black pepper to taste
1 tablespoon chopped chives or
   green onion
1 tablespoon chopped parsley

Scrape the carrots and beets and shred them and the peppers on a fine shredder. Peel the cucumber and shred on a coarse shredder. Cut the cabbage in strips with a sharp knife.

On a large platter, arrange cottage cheese and place vegetables in separate mounds around cheese. Serve with dressing made of sour cream, lemon juice, salt, pepper, chives and parsley.

Serves 6.

ORANGE AND ONION SALAD

3 large oranges,
   peeled and thinly sliced
2 to 3 sweet onions,
   sliced paper thin

2 heads romaine,
   broken into serving pieces
Basic French Dressing
   (page 152)
Rosemary

Just before serving, add oranges and onions to romaine. Toss with French dressing perfumed with rosemary.

Serves 8.

RUSSIAN SALAD

1 cup cold cooked green peas
1 cup cold cooked cut-up tiny
   green beans
1 cup cold cooked small-diced
   carrots
1 cup cold cooked small-diced
   potatoes
1 cup chopped onion

½ cup high-quality wine vinegar
½ cup olive oil
   Salt to taste
1 cup Mayonnaise (page 153)
   Lettuce
   Chopped parsley
   Pimiento strips
   Green pepper strips

Combine vegetables and pour over them vinegar and oil. Let them stand for 1 hour. Salt to taste. Blend well with mayonnaise. Arrange in a mound on a bed of lettuce or fill a large oiled mold with the salad and unmold it on lettuce. Top with a dollop of mayonnaise. Garnish with parsley, pimiento and green pepper.

Serves 6.

Note: The vegetables should be cooked quickly until just crisply tender.

POTATO SALAD

8 medium potatoes
1 cup olive oil
¼ cup wine vinegar
1 teaspoon salt
1 teaspoon freshly ground
   black pepper

½ cup finely chopped onion
½ cup finely chopped parsley
   Romaine
   Mayonnaise (page 153)

Boil potatoes in their jackets in salted water until just pierceable. While still warm, peel and cut into even slices. Marinate in oil, vinegar, salt and pepper. Chill overnight. Next day, add onion, parsley and additional oil and vinegar if needed. Serve on a bed of romaine in a large glass bowl. Have a bowl of mayonnaise on the side.

Serves 8.

RICE SALAD

2 cups rice
½ cup olive oil
¼ cup wine vinegar
1 teaspoon salt
1 teaspoon freshly ground
   black pepper
1 teaspoon tarragon
½ cup finely cut green pepper
½ cup finely cut pimiento

½ cup chopped parsley
1 cup chopped onion
1 cup chopped ripe tomato
1 cup chopped seeded
   cucumber
French dressing
Lettuce leaves
Sliced hard-cooked eggs
Sliced olives

Cook rice until just tender. While still hot, add olive oil, vinegar, salt, pepper and tarragon. Toss lightly to blend. Cool. When thoroughly cooled, add green pepper, pimiento, parsley, onion, tomato and cucumber. Blend well. Just before serving, dress with additional French dressing and arrange on lettuce leaves. Garnish with eggs and olives.

Serves 10.

BASIC FRENCH DRESSING

¼ cup wine vinegar or
   lemon juice
1 cup olive oil

Salt and freshly ground
   black pepper to taste

Combine all ingredients and blend well. This classic French dressing, or vinaigrette sauce, should be mixed just before using.

Other oils, such as peanut oil or corn oil, may be substituted for the olive oil, but the flavor will not be the same. Be sure your wine vinegar is the real thing; some on the market are imitations and are much too vinegary. If you like a little additional flavor, such as tarragon or some other herb, I suggest that you add the flavoring yourself to suit your taste instead of buying ready-flavored vinegars.

Makes 1¼ cups.

MAYONNAISE

---

2 egg yolks
  Salt to taste

½ teaspoon dry mustard
1 cup olive oil

There are several secrets to making good mayonnaise. First, use only good olive oil and the best fresh eggs. Second, have all ingredients at room temperature. And third, add the oil very slowly.

Select a shallow dish and use a silver fork for mixing. Start with the egg yolks, adding salt to taste and the dry mustard. Blend thoroughly with the fork. Then start adding the olive oil a few drops at a time, beating thoroughly all the while. If the mixture starts to curdle, start another batch with 1 egg yolk and some oil and gradually stir in the curdled mixture. If the dressing seems to be getting too thick, add a few drops of lemon juice or vinegar. Continue adding the oil and beating until all the oil is used up. Taste for seasoning. You may want to add more salt, some lemon juice or wine vinegar or perhaps some cayenne pepper or some more dry mustard.

This makes a rich, thick mayonnaise that is thoroughly delicious.

Makes about 1½ cups.

GREEN MAYONNAISE

---

1 cup Mayonnaise (above)
1 tablespoon finely chopped
  parsley
1 tablespoon finely chopped
  spinach
1 tablespoon finely chopped
  chives

1 tablespoon finely chopped
  fresh tarragon
1 tablespoon finely chopped
  fresh chervil
  Grated garlic

Combine the first 6 ingredients and flavor with a little garlic.

Makes about 1½ cups.

RUSSIAN DRESSING

---

1 cup Mayonnaise (page 153)
¼ cup chili sauce
1 teaspoon chopped onion

1 tablespoon chopped olives
1 hard-cooked egg, chopped

Combine all ingredients.

Makes about 1½ cups.

REMOULADE SAUCE

---

1 cup Mayonnaise (page 153)
1 teaspoon dry mustard
1 tablespoon finely chopped
   anchovies
1 tablespoon chopped parsley
1 clove garlic, grated
1 tablespoon capers

1 hard-cooked egg, chopped
Pinch tarragon
Chopped green olives
   (optional)
Horseradish (optional)
Chopped green pepper
   (optional)

Combine all ingredients.

Makes about 1½ cups.

10
SAUCES

BECHAMEL SAUCE

---

2 tablespoons butter
2 tablespoons flour
1 cup milk

Salt and freshly ground
   black pepper to taste

Blend butter and flour over low heat. Remove from heat or place over hot water. Add milk very slowly, blending all the while. Return to heat and cook, stirring constantly, until the sauce thickens and is perfectly smooth. Season with salt and pepper to taste. To make a thicker sauce, use 3 to 4 tablespoons flour.

Makes about 1 cup.

VELOUTE SAUCE

½ cup heavy cream
 2 egg yolks

1 cup Béchamel Sauce
   (above), made with meat,
   poultry, fish or vegetable
   stock instead of milk

Blend heavy cream with egg yolks. Add to béchamel sauce in the top of a double boiler over hot water. Stir until thickened but do not allow to boil—the eggs will scramble if you do.

Makes 1½ cups.

MORNAY SAUCE

---

1 cup Béchamel Sauce (left)

1 egg yolk

½ cup grated Gruyère or Cheddar cheese

Dry mustard

To cream sauce add egg yolk and cheese with just a touch of mustard. Stir over hot—not boiling—water until the cheese is melted and the sauce well blended.

Makes 1½ cups.

BEARNAISE SAUCE

---

3 chopped shallots

1 teaspoon chopped parsley

1 teaspoon tarragon

½ cup wine vinegar

4 egg yolks

½ cup butter, softened

Salt to taste

Cayenne pepper

Cook shallots, parsley and tarragon in wine vinegar until it is merely a glaze on the bottom of the pan. Strain the reduced liquid. Place a pottery bowl over—not in—hot water. Put in egg yolks and add the strained liquid a little at a time, stirring constantly, until the mixture thickens. Add half of the butter, a tablespoon at a time. Blend well. Add the remaining butter, again by tablespoons, and stir until it has the consistency of mayonnaise. Season with salt to taste and add just a bit of cayenne. Additional parsley and tarragon may be added.

Makes 1 cup.

SALSA FRIA

1 can (16 ounces) solid-pack tomatoes, drained and cut very fine
1 onion, finely chopped
1 can (4 ounces) green chilies, peeled and chopped
1 teaspoon oregano
2 tablespoons wine vinegar
1 tablespoon oil
Salt and freshly ground black pepper to taste
1 teaspoon coriander

Mix all the ingredients together thoroughly.

This cold Mexican sauce, a favorite of Elena Zelayeta's, is superb with meats. It is unbelievably good on hamburgers and barbecued dishes. Try it in place of catsup.

Makes about 2½ cups.

SAUCE DIABLE

2 cans (10½-ounce size) consommé
3 chopped shallots or green onions
¼ cup butter
¼ cup flour
2 teaspoons Worcestershire sauce
Juice of 1 lemon
Dash Tabasco sauce
2 teaspoons Dijon mustard

Cook consommé until reduced to 1 cup. Cook shallots in butter until wilted, then add flour, Worcestershire sauce, lemon juice, Tabasco sauce and mustard. Mix well and continue cooking as you add the reduced consommé. Stir until smooth and well blended.

This sauce is good with kidneys, mutton chops, liver and many other meats.

Makes 1 cup.

CURRY SAUCE

6 tablespoons butter
2 medium onions, finely
  chopped
2 cloves garlic, finely chopped
2 carrots, finely chopped
2 dried chili peppers, soaked,
  seeded and chopped
2 unpeeled apples, finely
  chopped

2 cups beef consommé or
  chicken broth
1 to 2 tablespoons curry
  powder
1 teaspoon salt
  Grated fresh ginger or
  chopped preserved ginger
½ cup coconut milk

Heat butter in a skillet and sauté onions, garlic, carrots, chili peppers and apples. Cover and simmer 15 minutes. Add consommé and re-cover. Simmer for about 45 minutes more.

Add curry powder according to taste, salt, a little ginger and coconut milk. (If this is not available, soak 1 cup grated coconut in 1 cup cream for 1 hour. Squeeze all the liquid out of the coconut and add to sauce.)

Bring the sauce to a boil, taste for seasoning and serve with any meat, fish or vegetable that you like in a curry dish.

Makes about 3 cups.

HORSERADISH CREAM

½ cup freshly grated
  horseradish

1 cup dairy sour cream or
  whipped heavy cream
  Salt to taste

Combine horseradish with sour cream. Salt to taste.

Makes about 1½ cups.

CREOLE SAUCE

½ cup minced onion
⅔ cup sliced mushrooms
⅔ cup minced green pepper
1 garlic clove, minced
¼ cup butter
2 cups canned tomatoes
1 cup condensed tomato soup
 Bay leaf

Parsley
Thyme
Whole cloves
1 teaspoon salt
¼ teaspoon freshly ground
 black pepper
¼ teaspoon paprika

Sauté onion, mushrooms, green pepper and garlic in butter until just tender. Add tomatoes, tomato soup and a bouquet garni of bay leaf, parsley, thyme and cloves. Blend in salt, pepper and paprika. Simmer gently for 20 minutes. Remove bouquet before serving.

Makes about 4 cups.

11
BREADS

ROLL DOUGH

¾ cup milk
¼ cup sugar
2¼ teaspoons salt
4½ tablespoons shortening
¾ cup water

1 package active dry yeast or
1 cake compressed yeast
4½ cups sifted enriched flour
(approximately)

Scald the milk and stir in the sugar, salt and shortening. Cool to lukewarm. Heat the water to warm, not hot (cool to lukewarm for compressed yeast), and pour into a good-size bowl. Sprinkle or crumble in yeast and stir until dissolved. Stir in lukewarm milk mixture and add 2¼ cups flour. Beat until smooth, then stir in just enough of the remaining flour to make a dough that is easy to handle. Shape into one of the variations below.

Variations

Pan Rolls: Divide roll dough in half and form each half into a roll about 12 inches long. Cut each roll into 12 equal pieces and form into smooth balls. Place balls about ¼ inch apart in greased shallow baking pans. Cover. Let rise in warm place, free from draft, until doubled in bulk. Uncover and brush lightly with melted butter or margarine. Bake in a preheated 375° oven for about 20 minutes.

Makes 24 rolls.

Tiny Rolls: Proceed as for Pan Rolls (above), except cut each 12-inch roll of dough into 24 equal pieces. Continue as above, baking in a preheated 375° oven for about 10 minutes.

Makes 48 rolls.

Bubble Loaf: Divide roll dough in half and form each half into a roll about 12 inches long. Cut each roll into 24 equal pieces and form into balls. Place a layer of balls about ½ inch apart in each of 2 greased loaf pans, 9x5x3 inches, or 1 9-inch tube pan. Brush lightly with melted butter or margarine. Arrange a second layer of balls on top of first. Cover. Let rise in warm place, free from draft, until dough has risen slightly higher than edge of pan. Uncover and brush again lightly with melted butter or margarine. Bake in a preheated 375° oven for about 30 minutes.

Makes 2 regular loaves or 1 ring loaf.

Curlicues: Divide roll dough in half and roll out each half into an oblong about 12x9 inches. Brush generously with melted butter or margarine. Cut each oblong into 12 equal strips about 1 inch wide. Hold one end of strip firmly and wind closely to form coil. Tuck end firmly underneath. Place about 2 inches apart on greased baking sheets. Cover. Let rise in warm place, free from draft, until doubled in bulk. Uncover and brush lightly with melted butter or margarine. Bake in a preheated 400° oven for about 15 minutes.

Makes 24 rolls.

Crescents: Divide roll dough into 3 equal pieces and roll each piece into a circle about 9 inches in diameter. Brush lightly with melted butter or margarine and cut each circle into 8 pie-shaped wedges. Roll up tightly, beginning at the wide end. Seal points firmly. Place on greased baking sheets about 2 inches apart with points underneath, then curve to form crescents. Cover. Let rise in warm place, free from draft, until doubled in bulk. Uncover and brush lightly with melted butter or margarine. Bake in a preheated 400° oven for about 15 minutes.

Makes 24 rolls.

Cloverleaf Rolls: Divide roll dough in half and form each half into a 9-inch roll. Cut each roll into 9 equal pieces and form each piece into 3 small balls. Place 3 balls in each section of greased muffin pans, 2¾x1¼ inches. Cover. Let rise in warm place, free from draft, until doubled in bulk. Uncover and brush lightly with melted butter or margarine. Bake in a preheated 400° oven for about 15 minutes.

Makes 18 rolls.

BRIOCHES

½ cup milk
½ cup butter or margarine
⅓ cup sugar
½ teaspoon salt
¼ cup water
1 package active dry yeast or
    1 cake compressed yeast

1 egg yolk, beaten
3 eggs, beaten
3¼ cups sifted enriched flour
1 egg white
1 tablespoon sugar

Scald the milk. Cool to lukewarm. Cream the butter thoroughly. Add sugar and salt gradually and cream together. Heat the water to warm, not hot (cool to lukewarm for compressed yeast), and pour into a good-size bowl. Sprinkle or crumble in yeast and stir until dissolved. Stir in lukewarm milk and butter mixture. Add egg yolk, eggs and flour; beat 10 minutes. Cover. Let rise in warm place, free from draft, about 2 hours or until more than doubled in bulk. Stir down and beat thoroughly. Cover tightly with waxed paper or aluminum foil and store in refrigerator overnight. Stir down and turn out onto floured board.

Divide dough into 2 pieces, one about 3 times the size of the other. Cut larger piece into 16 equal pieces and form into smooth balls. Place in well-greased muffin pans or fluted brioche molds, 2¾x1¾ inches. Cut smaller piece into 16 equal pieces and form into smooth balls. Make a deep indentation in center of each large ball and dampen slightly with cold water. Press a small ball into each indentation. Cover and let rise in warm place, free from draft, about 1 hour or until more than doubled in bulk. Combine egg white and sugar. Uncover brioches and brush with egg white mixture. Bake in a preheated 375° oven for about 20 minutes.

Makes 16 brioches.

Variations

Tiny Brioches: Divide dough into 2 unequal pieces, as above. Form larger piece into about 50 small balls, and smaller piece into an equal number of smaller balls. Assemble as above, placing in well-greased tiny muffin tins or fluted brioche molds. Proceed as above, baking for about 10 minutes in a preheated 375° oven.

Makes about 50 brioches.

Brioche Loaf: Divide dough in half and shape into 2 loaves. Place each in a greased 8½x4½x2½-inch loaf pan. Proceed as at left, baking for about 30 minutes in a preheated 375° oven or until loaves are golden brown and sound hollow when tapped.

Makes 2 loaves.

HOT BISCUITS

---

2 cups flour	1 teaspoon sugar
2 teaspoons double-acting baking powder	¼ cup butter, softened
½ teaspoon salt	¾ cup milk (approximately)

Sift together flour, baking powder, salt and sugar. Work butter into this mixture until it is thoroughly mixed with the dry ingredients. Toss with just enough milk to make a soft dough that can be easily handled. Put onto a floured board and pat or roll out, about ½ inch thick for fluffy biscuits, ¼ inch thick for crisper ones. Cut into 1½-inch rounds and place on a greased baking sheet. Bake in a preheated 425° oven for 15 to 20 minutes.

Makes about 24 biscuits.

Note: If you like thick, fluffy biscuits, pat or roll dough thicker and place biscuits close together on baking sheet; brush with butter before baking. But if you like them crisp, roll dough very thin and bake far apart; don't brush with butter.

CORN BREAD

¾ cup flour
2 teaspoons double-acting
   baking powder
¼ teaspoon salt
1 cup cornmeal

3 eggs, lightly beaten
¾ cup heavy cream
   (approximately)
½ cup butter, melted

Sift together flour, baking powder and salt. Add this mixture with cornmeal to eggs. Add just enough heavy cream to make a soft batter. Beat in the butter. Pour into a well-buttered 9x9-inch baking pan. Bake in a preheated 375° oven for 20 to 25 minutes or until the bread is nicely browned. It should be thin, crisp and hot.

HERBED FRENCH BREAD

1 large loaf French bread
½ cup butter, softened
½ cup chopped parsley
½ cup chopped chives
1 clove garlic, grated

2 tablespoons chopped fresh or
   1½ teaspoons dried basil
   (optional)
Toasted sesame seeds

Cut loaf in half lengthwise. Cream butter with parsley, chives, garlic and basil. Spread the bread with this mixture and sprinkle with sesame seeds. Press the halves of the loaf together. Place on a baking sheet in a preheated 350° oven for about 15 minutes. Cut in thick slices right through the loaf.

CHEESED MELBA TOAST

Cut thin slices of white or protein bread. Brush with soft butter and sprinkle with grated Parmesan cheese and a bit of paprika. Toast slowly in a preheated 250° oven until crisp and nicely browned.

JULE KAGA

1 cup milk	1½ teaspoons ground cardamom
½ cup sugar	½ cup raisins
1 teaspoon salt	¼ cup chopped citron
½ cup shortening	¼ cup chopped candied cherries
¼ cup water	¼ cup chopped almonds
2 packages active dry yeast or 2 cakes compressed yeast	Confectioners' sugar
	Water
4½ cups sifted enriched flour (approximately)	Blanched almonds
	Candied fruit

Scald the milk; stir in sugar, salt and shortening. Cool to lukewarm. Heat the water to warm, not hot (cool to lukewarm for compressed yeast), and pour into a good-size bowl. Sprinkle or crumble in yeast and stir until dissolved. Stir in lukewarm milk mixture. Add 2 cups flour and beat thoroughly. Cover and let rise in warm place, free from draft, until doubled in bulk, about 30 minutes. Stir down and stir in cardamom, raisins, citron, candied cherries and almonds. Stir in about 2½ cups more flour.

Turn out on lightly floured board. Knead until smooth and elastic. Place in greased bowl and brush with melted shortening. Cover and let rise in warm place, free from draft, until doubled in bulk, about 55 minutes. Punch down and form into round ball. Place on a large greased baking sheet. Cover and let rise in warm place, free from draft, until doubled in bulk, about 1 hour. Bake in a preheated 400° oven for 10 minutes. Reduce heat to 350° and continue baking for 40 minutes. Cool. Ice with a glaze made of confectioners' sugar and water; decorate with almonds and candied fruit.

KUGELHUPF

½ cup milk
½ cup sugar
½ teaspoon salt
¼ cup butter or margarine
¼ cup water
1 package active dry yeast or
   1 cake compressed yeast

2 eggs, beaten
2½ cups sifted enriched flour
   Fine bread crumbs
14 to 16 almonds, blanched
½ cup seedless raisins
½ teaspoon grated lemon peel

Scald the milk; stir in sugar, salt and butter. Cool to lukewarm. Heat the water to warm, not hot (cool to lukewarm for compressed yeast), and pour into a good-size bowl. Sprinkle or crumble in yeast and stir until dissolved. Stir in lukewarm milk mixture. Add eggs and flour. Beat vigorously about 5 minutes. Cover. Let rise in warm place, free from draft, until doubled in bulk, about 1½ hours.

Sprinkle bread crumbs over sides and bottom of a well-greased 1½-quart casserole or kugelhupf mold. Arrange almonds on bottom. Stir batter down; beat thoroughly. Stir in raisins and lemon peel. Turn into prepared casserole. Let rise in warm place until doubled in bulk, 1 hour. Bake in a preheated 350° oven for 50 minutes.

12
DESSERTS

HONEYED FIGS

---

1 pound dried figs
2 cups white wine
   (approximately)

½ cup honey
   Heavy cream or dairy
   sour cream

Soak figs for several hours in just enough wine to cover. Heat to the boiling point. Add honey and cook for 2 minutes. Chill. Serve with cream.

Serves 4.

STRAWBERRIES IN RED WINE

---

1 quart large strawberries
   Sugar to taste

2 cups dry red wine

Wash and hull strawberries and place in a serving bowl. Sprinkle with sugar to taste and add red wine. Let stand in a cold place about 10 minutes before serving.

Serves 4.

STRAWBERRIES ROMANOFF

---

2 quarts strawberries
   Sugar
1 cup orange juice

1 cup Grand Marnier
3 cups heavy cream, whipped

Sprinkle strawberries lightly with sugar. Add orange juice and Grand Marnier. Let the berries soak in this for about 1 hour. Just before serving, fold in whipped cream.

Serves 8.

BROILED PINEAPPLE AND APRICOTS ON SKEWERS

24 pineapple chunks
    (fresh, canned or frozen)
24 apricot halves
    (fresh, canned or frozen)

Butter
Brown sugar
Rum (optional)

Arrange pineapple chunks and apricot halves alternately on 6 skewers. Broil over charcoal or in the broiler, brushing with butter and sprinkling with brown sugar several times during the process. Serve hot and brown, with a dash of rum if desired.

Serves 6.

BROILED PEACHES WITH BOURBON

8 peach halves (fresh or canned)
   Brown sugar
   Butter

Cinnamon
¾ cup bourbon, warmed

Arrange the peach halves on a cookie sheet or other flat baking dish. Heap the centers with brown sugar, dot with butter and sprinkle with cinnamon. Place about 4 inches from broiler heat source and broil for 5 minutes or until the sugar is melted and the peaches slightly browned. Arrange the peaches on a serving dish that is flameproof and add about 1½ tablespoons warmed bourbon to each peach half. Flame as you bring to the table.

Serves 4.

BAKED APPLES

Core as many apples as you'll need servings and pare them down around the top about an inch. Place them in a casserole or baking dish with ½ inch water. Fill each one of the apples with about 2 tablespoons sugar or sugar with cinnamon mixed—or fill according to one of the variations below. Dot generously with butter and bake for 30 to 40 minutes in a preheated 350° oven, basting often with the syrup that forms in the dish. When done, the apples should be lightly glazed. Serve them either hot or cold, with heavy cream, whipped cream or sour cream.

Variations

Raisin-Nut Apples: Fill the centers with a mixture of plumped raisins (ones soaked in water or sherry to fullness), chopped nuts and honey. Spread the tops of the apples with additional honey.

Orange Apples: Add a tablespoon or so of grated orange rind to each ½ cup sugar used for filling the apples; baste with orange juice.

Applejack-Brown Sugar Apples: Fill the centers with a mixture of butter and brown sugar creamed together. Baste with applejack.

APPLES AU RHUM

---

4 large tart apples	½ cup water
1 orange	½ cup sugar
4 tablespoons peach jam or preserves	3 tablespoons rum
	Whipped cream

Peel and core apples and cut into halves. Place, cut sides up, in a casserole. Juice the orange and grate the rind. Blend together juice and rind, peach jam, water and sugar over low heat to make a syrup. When thickened, remove from heat and add rum. Pour over apples and bake in a preheated 350° oven for 30 minutes. Serve cold, with whipped cream.

Serves 8.

APPLE CRUNCH

4 large tart apples
¼ cup granulated sugar
1 cup light brown sugar
1 cup sifted flour

1 cup pecans, finely chopped
½ cup butter, softened
½ teaspoon cinnamon
  Whipped or heavy cream

Peel and core apples. Cut them into thin slices and place half of them in the bottom of a well-greased shallow baking dish or casserole. Sprinkle with granulated sugar and add remaining apples.

Now combine light brown sugar with flour and pecans. Cream butter and gradually work in flour mixture with cinnamon. When all is well blended, spread over the apples, pressing the edges down firmly. Gash the surface 2 or 3 times and bake in a preheated 350° oven for 50 minutes. Serve with cream. This tastes best when it's served straight from the oven.

Serves 8.

RUSSIAN APPLE PUDDING

1 large loaf stale whole wheat
  or pumpernickel bread,
  crumbed
½ cup butter
  Rind of 1 lemon, grated
  Peel of 1 large orange,
  cut into very small pieces

½ cup dry sherry
½ cup sugar
3 large apples, peeled and
  thinly sliced
  Dairy sour or sweet cream

Sauté crumbs in butter. Add lemon rind, orange peel, sherry and sugar. Make a layer of this crumb mixture in the bottom of a buttered baking dish. Add a layer of apples, sprinkle lightly with additional sugar, then alternate with crumbs and apples until the dish is full, ending with a layer of crumbs. Dot with butter and bake in a preheated 300° oven for 1 hour. Serve with cream.

Serves 6.

SPICED PUDDING

1 cup boiling water
1 cup brown sugar
¼ cup butter
1 cup granulated sugar
1 cup flour
1 rounded teaspoon
   baking powder
½ teaspoon ground cloves
½ teaspoon nutmeg

½ teaspoon cinnamon
½ teaspoon ground allspice
   Pinch salt
1 cup mixed dried fruits,
   chopped
1 cup chopped nuts
⅔ cup cream and milk, mixed
   Cognac Sauce (below)

Combine the water, brown sugar and butter in a flameproof baking pan and bring to a boil on top of the stove. Meanwhile, mix granulated sugar, flour, baking powder, spices, salt, dried fruits, nuts and cream and milk mixture. Pour this batter over the brown sugar and water mixture. Bake in a preheated 350° oven for about 30 minutes or until the pudding has puffed up a bit and browned. Serve with the sauce.

Serves 6.

Cognac Sauce

⅔ cup water
⅔ cup butter
1 cup brown sugar

½ teaspoon cornstarch, mixed
   with 2 tablespoons
   cold water
   Pinch salt
   Jigger Cognac

Bring water to a boil and add butter and brown sugar. Bring to a boil again and simmer for a few minutes. Add cornstarch and cook, stirring, until sauce thickens. Add salt and flavor with Cognac. Serve hot or cold.

Makes 1½ cups.

CREME BRULEE

2 cups heavy cream
6 egg yolks
¼ teaspoon salt

¼ cup granulated sugar
1 teaspoon vanilla
1 cup light brown sugar

Scald heavy cream in top of double boiler. Beat egg yolks until light and foamy. Add salt and granulated sugar and beat until sugar is dissolved. Pour hot cream slowly over eggs and blend well. Return to double boiler and continue cooking over hot—not boiling—water. Stir continuously until the mixture coats the spoon. Remove from heat and stir in vanilla.

Pour into a shallow casserole. Place, uncovered, in the refrigerator and chill overnight or at least 6 hours.

Before serving, remove from refrigerator and sprinkle the top with light brown sugar. Place immediately under broiler, 6 inches from heat, and broil until sugar melts. Don't let it burn. Return to refrigerator to let crust harden and leave until serving.

Serves 6 to 8.

CHOCOLATE MOUSSE

8 ounces semisweet chocolate
3 tablespoons strong coffee
¼ cup sugar
6 eggs, separated

3 tablespoons butter, softened
½ cup heavy cream
2 tablespoons sugar

In a small saucepan, melt the chocolate in the coffee over low heat. Add the sugar and stir until dissolved. Cool. Transfer the chocolate mixture to a mixing bowl and add the egg yolks and butter. Stir well. Whip the cream until stiff and add the sugar. Fold this into the chocolate mixture. Beat the egg whites until stiff and fold in. Chill for several hours or until the mousse is firm.

Serves 6 to 8.

BANANA PUDDING

12 small bananas
2 eggs, beaten
½ cup butter, melted
2 tablespoons dark rum
1 teaspoon ground nutmeg

Sugar to taste
½ cup flour
2 teaspoons baking powder
Whipped or heavy cream

Peel and mash bananas. Combine pulp with eggs, butter, rum, nutmeg and sugar to taste.

Sift flour with baking powder. Blend with banana mixture and pour into a buttered casserole. Bake in a preheated 400° oven until mixture is bubbly, about 10 minutes. Then reduce the heat to 275° and continue cooking until a silver knife inserted in the center of the pudding comes out clean, about 30 minutes. Cool before serving with cream.

Serves 6.

BREAD PUDDING

2 cups cubed soft bread
1 quart milk, scalded
2 eggs
⅓ cup sugar
½ teaspoon salt

¼ cup melted butter
1 tablespoon grated lemon peel
Vanilla extract to taste

Soak the bread in the milk for 15 minutes. Beat the eggs slightly and add the sugar and salt. When well blended, combine with the bread mixture and stir in the melted butter, lemon peel and vanilla. Pour into a buttered baking dish. Bake in a preheated 350° oven for 1¼ hours or until a silver knife will come out clean when inserted in the center of the dish.

Serves 6.

ORANGE BREAD PUDDING

7 slices white bread
Butter
1 tablespoon grated orange rind
1 tablespoon grated lemon rind
4 eggs

½ cup sugar
Juice of 1 lemon, plus
  enough orange juice to
  total 2 cups
Brandy Sauce (below)

Remove crusts from bread slices. Butter slices generously, break them into pieces and place in a greased casserole. Sprinkle bread with orange and lemon rinds. Beat eggs with sugar. Add orange-lemon juice and beat again. Pour over the bread and let stand 1 hour. Bake in a preheated 325° oven for 40 minutes. Serve with the sauce.

Serves 6.

Brandy Sauce

1 cup heavy cream
½ cup butter
4 egg yolks

1 cup sugar
Brandy to taste

Bring cream to a boil and place over hot—not boiling—water. Add butter. Beat egg yolks until lemon-colored. Gradually beat in sugar. Combine with hot cream and butter. Let thicken over hot water, stirring constantly. Just before serving, add brandy to taste. Serve hot.

Makes about 2½ cups.

LEMON RICE PUDDING

½ cup rice
1 quart milk
3 eggs, separated
1 tablespoon butter
10 tablespoons sugar

Grated rind and juice of
  1½ lemons
¼ teaspoon salt
Grated rind and juice of
  ½ lemon

Boil rice in milk until it is soft, about 15 minutes. Remove from heat and add beaten egg yolks, butter, 4 tablespoons sugar, rind and juice of 1½ lemons and salt. Let thicken over very low heat, stirring constantly. Pour into a casserole.

Beat egg whites until they stand up in stiff peaks. Gently fold in 6 tablespoons sugar and rind and juice of ½ lemon. Top casserole with this. Brown in a preheated 350° oven for 15 minutes. Cool. The pudding thickens as it gets cooler.

Serves 6.

UPSIDE-DOWN FRUIT TART

½ to 1 cup butter
½ cup sugar
4 large apples, peeled, cored
  and sliced very thin
  Sugar

Butter
Rich tart pastry for a
  one-crust pie
Whipped cream or
  hard sauce

Spread a 9-inch metal pie plate with butter. Add sugar. Caramelize the sugar and butter over a low flame. Add a layer of apples, arranged in a pleasant pattern, then a sprinkling of sugar, then dots of butter, then more apples and sugar and butter until pan is piled high in the center. Cover this with the rolled-out tart pastry. Do not press edges against rim of plate. Bake in a preheated 375° oven for about 35 minutes or until the crust is nicely browned, the apples are cooked through and the syrup is thick and caramely. Turn pie out on serving plate as for upside-down cake. Serve warm, with whipped cream.

Serves 6 to 8.

PLUM TART

Pastry for one-crust pie
Sugar
8 to 10 ripe plums or
    Italian prunes
1 cup sugar
Cinnamon
Butter
Sweetened whipped cream

Line a 9-inch pie tin with your favorite pie crust. Sprinkle crust lightly with sugar. Cut plums in half and remove seeds. Arrange skin sides up in pie shell until it is well filled. Now add sugar and sprinkling of cinnamon. Dot with butter. Bake in a preheated 450° oven for 10 minutes. Reduce heat to 350° and continue baking until plums are tender, 15 to 20 minutes. Serve warm, with whipped cream.

Serves 6.

LINZER TORTE

1 cup butter, softened
2 cups sifted flour
¼ teaspoon salt
1 cup confectioners' sugar
1 cup ground almonds
½ teaspoon cinnamon
¼ teaspoon allspice
1 teaspoon cocoa
    Juice and grated rind of
    ½ lemon
3 egg yolks
2 cups raspberry jam
1 egg white, lightly beaten

Knead together first 10 ingredients. When thoroughly blended, chill. Then roll two-thirds of the dough ¼ inch thick and line a 9-inch pie plate or spring form pan, giving the dough a good edge. Spread dough generously with raspberry jam. Roll remaining dough into strips ¼ inch wide and place over jam, making a lattice design. Place one wide strip around torte edge. Paint dough with egg white. Bake in a preheated 350° oven for 45 to 55 minutes. When cool, fill squares formed by lattice with more jam. Sprinkle with confectioners' sugar.

Serves 8.

CHOCOLATE TORTE

1 cup flour
Pinch salt
2 teaspoons baking powder
3 squares (3 ounces)
   unsweetened chocolate
1 cup milk

4 eggs, separated
1½ cups sugar
1 teaspoon vanilla
1 cup heavy cream, whipped
   Helen's Fabulous Frosting
   (below)

Sift flour 3 times with salt and baking powder. Melt chocolate in milk over hot water or in a saucepan, stirring constantly. Cool slightly. Beat egg yolks until light and foamy. Gradually beat in sugar. Add chocolate-milk mixture, flour mixture and vanilla. Beat egg whites until stiff and fold into batter. Pour into a well-buttered 8-inch spring form pan. Bake in a preheated 350 to 375° oven for about 40 minutes or until a tester comes out dry. Remove from spring form. When cool, split and fill with whipped cream. Frost top and sides with Helen's Fabulous Frosting.

Serves 8 to 10.

Helen's Fabulous Frosting

1 package (5 ounces)
   semisweet chocolate

½ cup dairy sour cream
   Salt

Melt chocolate over hot water. Combine with sour cream. Add a little salt and stir until smooth.

STRAWBERRY ROLL

6 eggs, separated
6 tablespoons sugar
3 tablespoons sifted flour
   Pinch salt

1 teaspoon vanilla
   Butter
2 cups crushed strawberries
1 cup heavy cream, whipped

Combine egg yolks with 4 tablespoons sugar. Beat until thick and lemon-colored. Beat egg whites until stiff.

Gradually and carefully fold flour, salt, vanilla, then egg whites into yolk-sugar mixture. Butter a jelly roll pan, 12x18 inches. Line it with paper, then butter paper. Spread cake mixture over bottom of pan. Bake in a preheated 350° oven for 12 to 13 minutes.

Remove from oven and sprinkle with 1 tablespoon sugar. Loosen from pan and turn out, sugared side down, on waxed paper. Remove paper from bottom of cake carefully. Sprinkle cake with 1 tablespoon sugar and spread with crushed strawberries. Roll up from the wide edge. When cake is cooled, cover with whipped cream.

Serves 8 to 10.

CHOUX PASTE

1 cup water	1 cup flour
½ cup butter	3 or 4 eggs
Pinch salt	

Boil water in a heavy saucepan. Add butter. When butter is melted, add salt and flour. Stir vigorously until paste is a heavy ball in the center of the pan. Remove from heat, add 1 egg and beat well. Add another egg and beat in thoroughly. Add a third egg and beat until dough is waxy and glossy. If eggs are small- or medium-size, a fourth egg might be necessary to make a paste stiff enough to stand alone. Shape and cook as directed below.

For Fritters or Pets de Nonne: Drop by spoonfuls into deep fat heated to 370° and fry until brown and puffy. Roll in sugar or serve with hot fruit sauce.

For Puffs: Drop by spoonfuls onto a lightly buttered baking sheet. Bake in a preheated 400° oven for 10 minutes. Reduce heat to 350° and continue baking until puffs are well baked and thoroughly dried. Be certain they are thoroughly baked; otherwise they will fall and become dull and soggy. (Note that the puffs can be made in any size: Drop very tiny ones from a coffee spoon for profiteroles, use a teaspoon for hors d'oeuvres puffs, use a tablespoon for cream or ice cream puffs. If you are adept with a pastry tube, you can use it to great advantage with choux paste.)

POUND CAKE

2 cups butter, softened
3 cups sugar
9 eggs
4 cups sifted flour

Dash salt
Mace
¼ cup Cognac

Cream together butter and sugar until light and creamy. Beat in eggs, one at a time. When all eggs are added, fold in flour gently, spoonful by spoonful. Flavor with salt, a little mace and Cognac. Pour into 2 buttered 8½x4½x2½-inch loaf tins or into a buttered 9-inch tube pan. Bake in a preheated 300° oven for about 1½ hours or until a wooden pick inserted in the center of the cake comes out clean.

Serves 16 to 20.

CHOCOLATE CREPES

1 cup less 2 tablespoons flour
Pinch salt
¼ cup sugar
3 eggs
1 teaspoon vanilla

2 tablespoons Cognac
⅔ cup milk (approximately)
Sugar
Grated sweet chocolate
Whipped cream

Sift together flour, salt and sugar. Mix in eggs, adding them one at a time. (An electric mixer at low speed is perfect for this process.) Add vanilla and Cognac. Gradually add milk until batter is consistency of thick cream. Allow batter to rest for 1 to 2 hours.

Butter a 6-inch skillet well, pour in a little batter and tip the pan so batter runs all over the bottom. These cakes are supposed to be thin. Turn once and brown the other side. Place first crepe on a heated serving plate and sprinkle with sugar and grated chocolate; place another pancake on top of this and repeat process until there are about 12 pancakes on the pile. Cut pile into wedges and serve with whipped cream.

Serves 4.

SCOTCH SHORTBREAD

2 cups butter, softened
1 cup confectioners' sugar
4 cups sifted flour
  Pinch salt

1 teaspoon baking powder
  Candied angelica or citron
  Candied cherries

Mix together butter, sugar, flour, salt and baking powder with your hands. Knead the dough until thoroughly blended and crackly. To be traditional, divide the dough into 4 pieces and roll each out into a circle about ⅜ inch thick. Place circles on an ungreased baking sheet. Frill the edges with your fingers and prick the centers with a fork. For decoration, make a wreath of leaves cut from angelica and add a few candied cherries here and there. Bake in a preheated 350° oven until cakes are straw-colored, about 20 minutes. Serve whole, letting your guests break off little bits.

WINE JELLY

2¼ cups cold water
 ½ cup sugar
    Rind of 1 tangerine,
      thinly cut
    Rind of 1 lemon, thinly cut
 3 cloves
 1 small stick cinnamon

2 envelopes unflavored
    gelatin, soaked in a
    little cold water
  Juice of 1½ lemons
1¼ cups Madeira
  Heavy cream

Place water in a saucepan with sugar, tangerine rind, lemon rind, cloves and cinnamon. Bring to a boil, then reduce heat and simmer for 10 minutes. Dissolve gelatin in the hot mixture. Add lemon juice and Madeira. Strain into a 1½-quart ring mold that has been rinsed in cold water. Cool, then chill until set. Unmold onto a cold platter. Serve with heavy cream, sweetened lightly and flavored with a little Madeira.

Serves 6.

CHESTNUTS FLAMBE

2 jars (8-ounce size) whole chestnuts in syrup

⅓ cup Cognac, warmed

Heat the chestnuts with their syrup over a low flame until syrup is just at boiling point. Remove to a serving dish and add Cognac, igniting it just as the dish is carried to the table.

Serves 6.

INDEX